AF539833

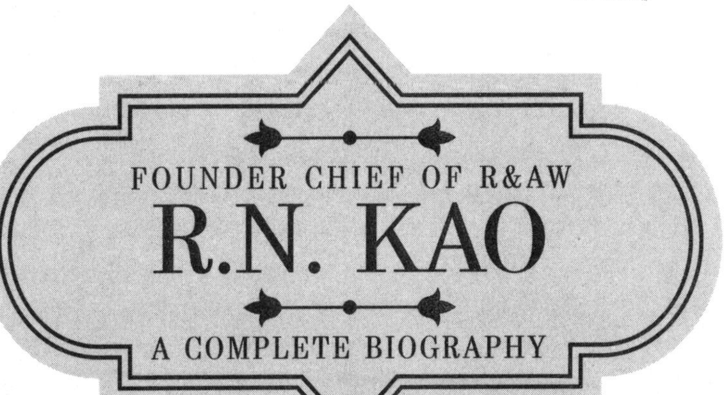
FOUNDER CHIEF OF R&AW
R.N. KAO
A COMPLETE BIOGRAPHY

VIPUL KUMAR

PRABHAT
PRAKASHAN

Published by

PRABHAT PRAKASHAN PVT. LTD.
4/19 Asaf Ali Road,
New Delhi-110 002 (INDIA)
e-mail: prabhatbooks@gmail.com

ISBN 978-93-5562-657-8
R.N. KAO: A COMPLETE BIOGRAPHY
by Vipul Kumar

Edition
2026

Price
₹ 300 (Rupees Three Hundred Only)

Printed at
R-Tech Offset Printers, Delhi

Author's Note

In the hidden corridors of India's intelligence world, a legendary figure emerges - Rameshwar Nath Kao the Spymaster of India, better known as R.N. Kao. Born in Varanasi in 1918, Kao's journey was destined to be one of immense significance to the nation he loved. A member of a distinguished family, his sense of duty and commitment to serving India were evident from a young age.

Through the Indian Administrative Service (IAS), Kao embarked on a distinguished career in the government, but it was his appointment as the head of the Aviation Research Centre (ARC) in 1968 that set the stage for his most influential role. Tasked with founding India's external intelligence agency, Kao went on to become the visionary architect of the Research and Analysis Wing (RAW) - an agency that would shape India's national security landscape profoundly.

R.N. Kao's contributions to India's intelligence capabilities were immeasurable. Under his astute leadership, RAW became a force to be reckoned with, working diligently in the shadows to safeguard the nation's interests. From the successful intelligence operations during the Indo-Pakistani War of 1971 to the annexation of Sikkim into India, Kao's strategic acumen and dedication were paramount in shaping India's destiny.

Despite his monumental achievements, R.N. Kao remained a private and humble figure, rarely seeking recognition for his work.

The secrecy that shrouded his life added to the aura of mystery that surrounded him, leaving much of his legacy hidden from public view.

As we delve into the life and accomplishments of R.N. Kao, we pay tribute to the silent hero whose unwavering dedication to the nation and remarkable contributions to its security continue to inspire generations. His profound impact on India's intelligence community endures, and his legacy remains etched in the annals of the nation's history.

It is with utmost humility and respect that I present this biography, an earnest effort to pay tribute to a man who dedicated his life to safeguarding our nation's interests and securing its future.

In writing this book, I hope to bring to light the remarkable achievements and the lesser-known aspects of R.N. Kao's life, allowing his story to inspire and resonate with readers from all walks of life. May this tribute serve as a reminder of the profound impact one individual can have on the course of history.

❑

Contents

Introduction

The military shadows of India keep their secrets deep and close to their chests. Most people know very little about these covert operations, and those who do, are increasingly under fire for their actions and for the mistakes that could cost them everything. Still, these men and women undertake highly dangerous jobs in service to their nation. These sacrifices are possible only because of the strength of the military community in India, which shares its collective memories with the families at home and respects those who have fallen on the battlefield without revealing anything that could put other operations or agents at risk. The people of India may not understand exactly what these operatives do, but they know that their country would not be safe without them.

The fact that we still know nothing about the spy world in India is a story of success for them and their work. Every man who takes part in these covert operations performs his duties invisibly and disappears into thin air as soon as his tasks are finished. This secrecy is crucial for the safety and security of the country, as any leak or exposure could compromise the ongoing operations and endanger the lives of those involved. However, it also makes it difficult for the public to fully appreciate and understand the sacrifices made by these brave individuals in service to their nation. But then, there are a few of them that are such valuable assets for the country that if we do not mention them and only focus on taking the legacy forward to the future generation of the country, we will miss out on various opportunities for various reasons. One such name is that of Mr. Rameshwar Nath Kao. Due to the sheer magnitude of his contributions to the nation, it isn't easy to know where to begin, as he has done so much for the country. Mr. Rameshwar Nath Kao was the founder of India's external intelligence agency, the Research and Analysis Wing (RAW), and played a crucial role in strengthening India's national security. This book will only reveal the very tip of the iceberg in terms of his contribution for the country. Still, his legacy is an inspiration for generations to come, and his contributions for the country will always be remembered with immense gratitude. Despite the numerous contributions that Mr. R.N. Kao made to India's national security, many of his exploits and texts have yet to be made public, as he himself has left instructions about each of his exploits, and there are a great many texts and escapades associated with him that are still kept under covers. Among these secret texts, the most anticipated ones are the papers related to the assassination of Indira Gandhi which will be revealed by 2025, as per R.N. Kao's precise instructions.

The book is a tribute to Mr. Kao's life and achievements, and sheds light also on his incredible journey from being a humble civil servant to the founder of RAW. It touches upon the problems he encountered when starting the agency, and how his vision and leadership helped him solve them.

The life of R.N. Kao was a well-kept secret, and as a result, the information written in this book may not be as accurate. This is because even if you try to find the information online, you won't see much of him there. This book is based on the personal experiences of his family, friends, and other people associated with him. However, despite the potential inaccuracies, the book provides valuable insights into the life and work of R.N. Kao, who is widely regarded as a pioneer in the field of intelligence gathering and analysis in India. It sheds light on his leadership style and his contributions to the development of India's intelligence community.

He was rarely photographed or interviewed by any of the journalists. Being at the top of the ladder in bureaucracy and the most trusted man of Jawaharlal Nehru, the Prime Minister of India of his time, it was surprising to see him always standing in the shadows.

It was the time when India was celebrating the 25th birth anniversary of Bangladesh in the year 1996. During an event, there were delegates sitting on the stage, and the media was interviewing them. The delegates shared their thoughts on the strong bond between India and Bangladesh and how it has grown over the years. The media asked questions about the future prospects of this relationship and the steps that could be taken to further strengthen it. During all this time, there was one man sitting on the very last bench in the room, and a journalist happened to recognize him. The man had an attractive and pleasing personality that was hard to ignore. After recognizing him, the journalist approached him and asked, "Why are you sitting here, sir? You ought to have been up there on that stage because, if it hadn't been for you, the operation that took place in 1971 would never have been successful." This prompted him to respond with a smile, "I did nothing. It was a complete and total group effort." However, he was disappointed with the fact that he was recognized by someone.. He was so shaken up and embarrassed by what had happened that he bolted out of the room the moment the event was over. It seemed like he didn't want to take any credit for the group's effort but rather preferred to remain anonymous. Such was the temperament of R.N. Kao.

In 1971, during the war between India and Pakistan, R.N. Kao and his team demonstrated that India's RAW intelligence agency was among the best in the world. Even before Pakistan attacked India, RAW had already given us every piece of information we required to win the war, so we were prepared for their assault when it came. Kao's humility and dedication to his work were remarkable traits that set him apart from others in the intelligence community. India's victory in the 1971 war was due to his leadership and the hard work of his team. This solidified RAW's reputation as a world-class intelligence agency.

After the victory in 1971, Indira Gandhi had such faith in RAW that she gave Kao responsibility for every other problem that arose in the country. Kao, on the other hand, had such faith in his team that when Indira Gandhi entrusted him with the mission of integrating Sikkim into India in 1975, he took only four officers with him on the mission and managed to carry it out flawlessly. The success of RAW under Kao's leadership continued even after the 1971 war, as he oversaw several covert operations in neighbouring countries to gather intelligence and protect India's interests.

Kao was widely regarded as the best-dressed man in the entire bureaucracy at the time, as he frequently sported suits that had been manufactured in London. His presence and his physique made him a subject of admiration and envy at the same time by many people.. Kao's leadership and successful operations earned him immense respect and appreciation, and he became a legendary figure in the world of Indian intelligence. He retired from RAW in 1977, but continued to be involved in various government committees and advisory roles until his death in 2002.

People, who knew Kao and had worked with him in the past, always used to say that he had a unique strategy for solving each problem that he encountered. He was not the type of man who could be contained within the confines of documents and records. He was the kind of man who delighted in thinking things through and always managed to come out on top in every arena. He was always considering the direction that the future should take and how it could be of use to the nation.

R.N. Kao was born into a family that belonged to a higher social class, but it did not guarantee an easy childhood. His life was nothing less than a roller coaster ride from those early days, until the day he became the chief and a founding member of one of the best intelligence agencies in the world.

❑

Introduction Extended

When Malini Kao (his wife) was first introduced to R.N. Kao and asked about his name, he replied that it was Ramji. At the time, she had no idea that his name was not just a simple identifier, but a reflection of his personality as well. In fact, Kao embodied the qualities and characteristics that one might associate with the name, Ramji.

Ramji is a name that is often associated with Lord Rama, a revered figure in Hindu mythology known for his courage, righteousness, and sense of duty. Kao, too, was known for his unwavering commitment to his work and his country. He was a man of great integrity and a strong moral compass, which made him an excellent choice for roles that required immense responsibility and trust.

Kao's physical appearance and demeanor also seemed to reflect the qualities associated with the name Ramji. He carried himself with an air of calm and quiet confidence, and his measured words and actions were a testament to his wisdom and prudence.

In many ways, Kao's name was a fitting introduction to his character and his contributions for his country. It was a reminder of the values and ideals that he stood for, and the example that he set for others to follow.

R.N. Kao was a man of many facets, with interests and habits that extended beyond his professional life. He had a deep knowledge and appreciation of Hindu mythology, with a particular fondness for the Bhagavad Gita and the Ramayana. His punctuality was also well-known among those close to him. He was precise in his daily routine, eating his breakfast at 9 a.m., lunch at 1:30 p.m., and dinner at 9 p.m. When he requested his family to get ready by a certain time, they knew that they should be ready several minutes beforehand.

Despite his busy schedule, Kao enjoyed hosting parties for his friends and colleagues, where he would serve food and drinks to his guests. Although he himself was a vegetarian and teetotaller, he would always make alcohol available for his guests. His wife, Malini, was also an excellent cook and would often prepare delicious meals for the guests.

Kao was known for his impeccable sense of style as well. During the winter months, he could often be seen wearing three-piece suits; while in the summer, he preferred to wear khadi bush shirts. His attention to detail extended even to his personal life, and he made sure that everything he wore was well-fitted and of the highest quality.

Kao's devotion to his family was also evident in his living arrangements. He and his younger brother shared a home with their respective wives and children. They named their house Saketa, after Ayodhya, the mythical city of Lord Rama. The two brothers lived together like Rama and Lakshmana, and their close bond was a reflection of the importance Kao placed upon family and relationships.

Hormis Tharakan, who served as the head of RAW from 2005 to 2007, recounted an incident from 1998 when he had met R.N. Kao for the last time before being posted to another location. Kao had graciously invited Hormis and his wife Molly to their home, where they were warmly received by Malini with a broad smile. However, Kao who was known for his punctuality, showed his displeasure that Hormis and Molly were running late by 15 minutes due to traffic.

Despite his annoyance, Kao remained the gracious host and offered Hormis a scotch, while he himself drank a soft drink. Hormis would remember this incident fondly, as it was a testament to Kao's character; even in the face of minor irritations, he remained polite and courteous.

Sankaran Nair, who succeeded R.N. Kao as the second Chief of RAW in 1977, also had a memorable encounter with Kao that displayed his true character. Nair shared that Kao was the kind of person who would never harm even his worst enemy, and always put others before himself.

Nair recalled an incident when an ex-colleague who used to spread rumours about Kao approached him for help. Despite the past animosity, Kao readily agreed to help his former colleague without any hesitation. When Nair questioned Kao's decision to help someone who had spoken ill of him, Kao replied that rumours could not harm him, but if he failed to help his colleague in need, it would harm his own mental health. Nair smiled at his reply and teased him to sit in the Himalayas in a cave and become a saint.

Nair and Kao may have had different personalities, but it is not uncommon for individuals with contrasting traits to work well together in achieving a common goal. While Nair may have disapproved of Kao's saintly nature, it is evident that both of them had mutual respect for each other, and worked together to build RAW from the ground up. It is possible that the success of RAW was not solely based on their individual personalities, but rather a combination of their unique strengths and perspectives.

Ultimately, it is team effort and collective work that leads to the success of any organization.

Achala's reminiscence of her father, R.N. Kao, sheds light on his creative interests and love for nature. Kao's passion for wood carving was evident in his masterpieces, which were kept in the house. His love for nature extended beyond wood carving, as he was also fond of playing with clay and stone. Kao's love for flowers was also notable, as he ensured that the flowers at home were changed twice a day. His appreciation for beauty and nature seems to have been an integral part of his personality, which is reflected in his creative pursuits and attention to detail.

After R.N. Kao retired, he was able to devote more time to his hobby of sculpting, which became increasingly addictive for him. He often visited Garhi village in Delhi, where he met many local artists, and developed a special bond with a young artist named Mohammad Sadiq. Together, they worked on many sculpting projects. Today, Sadiq lives in London, but he still maintains contact with Kao's family.

Kao's protective behaviour towards his daughter, Achala, was not uncommon for someone working in the intelligence field. Given the sensitive nature of his job, it was natural for him to take extra precautions to ensure the safety of his loved ones. His daily routine of asking about Achala's plans was perhaps a way to keep track of her movements, and ensure that she was never alone and vulnerable to any potential threats.

This level of protection may have seemed excessive to Achala at the time, but she later understood that it was necessary for her safety. Being in the intelligence field, Kao was well-aware of the risks and dangers that came with the job, and it was his responsibility to ensure the safety of his family.

Despite this, Kao's love for his daughter was undoubtedly a major factor in his protective behaviour, and he likely would have gone to great lengths to keep her safe regardless of his job.

The legacy of R.N. Kao still lives on even after his demise, and his family continues to receive compliments for the work he had done and for the kind of character he possessed. People still speak highly of him and share stories of his greatness with his family.

It is not unusual for people to stop Kao's wife and share their admiration for her late husband. She feels humbled by all the praise and recognition that is bestowed upon him even after all these years.

One incident that Kao's son-in-law recalls is particularly touching. He was once recognized as the son-in-law of R.N. Kao by a senior citizen who immediately started sobbing uncontrollably, and began to praise Kao for various things. This was the kind of respect and admiration people had for Kao.

Kao was a man of such extraordinary character and accomplishments, that even in a crowded room, he stood out. This was exemplified during a visit by the Dalai Lama to India, where Kao was among the audience members invited to welcome him. Despite his reservations about public attention, Kao attended the event, taking a seat in the rows at the back to avoid being the centre of attention. However, his fame and reputation preceded him, and when the Dalai Lama entered the room, he immediately recognized Kao, and made a beeline for him. The spiritual leader greeted Kao warmly, shaking his hand and addressing him by name, much to the surprise of many in the audience who had no idea who Kao was. Suddenly, all eyes turned to Kao, who was overwhelmed by the sudden attention and quickly became embarrassed. Despite his discomfort, Kao remained composed and polite during the ceremony. However, he left early, unable to cope with the scrutiny and the constant stares of those around him.

❑

Early Life

Motilal Nehru, who earned his wealth in the Banaras-Allahabad region after migrating from Kashmir, and later, as the name of Pandit Nehru (Jawaharlal Nehru) became a household name, many Kashmiri Pandits began to migrate to the Banaras-Allahabad region in the hope of gaining the name and fame while doing business or getting the education that could help them grab top-level jobs in the Indian bureaucracy. The migration of Kashmiri Pandits to the Banaras-Allahabad region continued even after independence, and many of them went on to occupy high positions in the Indian government.

At this time, both P.N. Haksar and another young Kashmiri Pandit, who was about two to three years younger than Haksar, were going to the well-known Allahabad University to educate themselves. It was sometime between the years 1929 and 1935. The young Kashmiri Pandit was none other than R.N. Kao himself, and the pair of Haksar and Kao was destined to play many significant roles in the early days of independent India. People had the misconception that Nehru favoured Haksar and Kao because they were members of the Kashmiri Pandit community; however, the truth was that both of them were thorough with their jobs and were never hesitant to advise the Prime Minister of India when things were not going in the nation's favour. People who criticized Nehru for choosing his favourites for the top position in the government, later realized that the choices that he made for the country's intelligence unit were the best ones, and there was no one better than Kao to lead RAW, which was to be to founded in 1968. Haksar and Kao were known for their dedication towards their work, and their contributions to the nation were immense.

For Kao, working for the government was a way to carry on the family legacy. After finishing his education in the late 1870s, his grandfather, Kedar Nath Kao, became a deputy collector for the British Raj, and was stationed in the province of Banaras. He held this position for the duration of his career. After that, Dwarika Nath Kao, the younger of Kedar Nath Kao's two sons and the father of R.N. Kao, also became deputy collector, following in the footsteps of his own father. R.N. Kao followed his family tradition and joined the Indian Administrative Service (IAS) in 1947. However, he later shifted to the Intelligence Bureau (IB) and was afterwards selected as the first Chief of India's external intelligence agency, the Research and Analysis Wing (RAW).

When Kao was born in the year 1918, his father was 24 years old, according to the notes that Kao wrote about his boyhood and childhood memories.. The death of Kao's father occurred when he was just 29 years old—long before Kao could recall what his father looked like, or how he behaved. When this happened, Kao was only 5 years old. The death of Kao's father was a significant loss for his family, and in order to ensure the family's survival, Kao's uncle, Triloki Nath Kao, made the decision to relocate to Baroda with all of his relatives. There was a chemical industry which was operated and managed by Triloki Kao. The move to Baroda brought new opportunities for Kao's family, and Triloki's chemical industry proved to be a successful venture. Despite the tragedy of losing his father at a young age, Kao was able to grow up in a stable and prosperous environment, thanks to his uncle's leadership. Gujarati was easy for him to pick up because he had spent a significant portion of his youth in Baroda. Triloki Nath raised his own family of four children—three boys and three girls—in the same home as Kao and his own brother, and as a result, Kao had several happy memories from his childhood. As his uncle's factory started to fail on multiplefronts, the economic state of Triloki Nath worsened, which eventually forced Kao's mother to take her children to Unnao, where her brother lived.

After a year in Unnao, the family relocated once again, this time to Banaras. They stayed as tenants in the home of Babu Durga Prasad, a powerful city official. He was the first of many men who came into Kao's life, and had a significant influence on him. Babu Durga Prasad was wealthy, and he enjoyed classical music, which he heard and played on his own instruments. He also enjoyed working on old clocks, and this passion could be seen on the top floor of the house, which appeared to be a graveyard for old clocks. Many of them were valuable and rare collections. Kao was fascinated by Babu Durga Prasad's love for classical music and old clocks.

After spending one year in Banaras, they had to relocate once again to Baroda. Kao, in his own writing, reveals that his childhood was not a very pleasant one. The passing of his father at a young age and watching his mother carry all the responsibility alone, moving from one place to another quite frequently, left a lasting impression on his psyche. And then, the school days at Baroda were also quite disheartening because he understood nothing of Gujarati in the early days, and English was the only medium he knew to converse with the other children, which was ridiculed by others. He also recalled that he was gaining weight during these years, and people nicknamed him the 'brown cow' because they mispronounced the word 'Kao' as 'cow'. He recalled that his mother would give him money so that he could purchase his lunch from the school canteen. However, as he was afraid of the other students, he avoided going to the canteen by himself. He would have his servants bring him lunch, and then he would go off to a quiet corner of the room to eat it by himself. Even as an adult, he had trouble getting used to the idea of eating at food stands on the side of the road because he was still plagued by the anxieties associated with eating in public settings.

R.N. Kao had a great deal of affection for both his mother and his grandmother. It was quite enjoyable for him to listen to either one of them talk about his father. Years later, he found out that his father had taught him to wear nice clothes. This was something he had gotten from his father. He was also strikingly handsome, and loved to make the most expensive sartorial choices. In addition, he had a hazy recollection of his father, but it was not one that was significant enough to be remembered. During those times, his father had stomach pain that kept him in bed and made it hard for him to do his day-to-day tasks. It went on for close to three months before it finally took his life. He also remembered that after the passing of his father, there were some days when he did nothing but watch people on the road, while sitting near his room's window and thinking nothing at all.

The struggle to meet ends continued for R.N. Kao's mother as thetimeswere difficult for his uncle. His factory had shut down, and in the meantime, he changed his field from a chemical factory to a cement company. There as well, he suffered lossses. The family then moved to Bombay, but there too, the stay was quite short. The Ramakrishna Mission's hostel in Villa Parle had to be the new home for the cousins and R.N. Kao. That was the period when he Kao found his new interest, practicing yoga. He wanted to lose the extra baggage on his body, and in the hope of losing weight, he started to put his time and interest into yoga. This was also the time when he started reading about Swami Vivekananda, and his writing fascinated him tremendously. His love for yoga, which ignited during his one-year stay at the hostel, stayed with him till the end of his life. Kao's interest in yoga and Swami Vivekananda's writing had a profound impact on his life. He continued to practice yoga, and was known to have incorporated its principles into his work as a spy and intelligence officer.

The financial condition of the Kao family kept on worsening, and that was the reason for the relocation of R.N. Kao. He then, along with his cousin, moved to Uttar Pradesh as they both got admission to Lucknow University for their Bachelor's degrees. As R.N. Kao recalls in his writings, this was the period when he started gaining interest in Indian history. As his subjects, he chose Indian History, and there he started to get intrigued by the ways India had developed over the course of time; and while studying he developed a deep bond with his motherland.

As he was reading books on Indian history, his interest led him to read about Indian architecture as well. There, he became captivated by various temples and their cultural background. Clay modelling became an outlet for him to explore his fascination with architecture and statues. He spent hours creating intricate models of temples and statues, which helped him in understanding the complexities of Indian architecture. Through his clay modelling, he discovered a new way to connect with his cultural heritage and express his creativity. He enjoyed every aspect of his academic life in Allahabad for the first two years, where he experimented on himself by taking various courses, and found his niche in English writing and speaking. This was the first time he had been recognized for his speaking abilities. Later at the University, he participated in English debates, and one of the best moments for him was winning first place in an inter-university debate in Allahabad in 1939. He discovered that he was very good at putting his words, facts, and ideas out there without reservations. He was encouraged by his teachers to take English Literature at Allahabad University during his Master's degree, so he enrolled without any hesitation. In addition, he began preparing for competitive exams because he desired to do something exceptional, and knew that only hard work would enable him to achieve his goals. When he was studying for the exams, he had a very strict schedule. He used to get up at 3 a.m. and work for eight hours straight, with only a few brief breaks. He desired to break the vicious financial cycle that had befallen upon his family, and carry on the legacy of his father and grandfather.

Those were the days when his mother gave him 50 rupees to cover all of his monthly expenses. This included tuition fees of 12 rupees and a hostel room fee of 8 rupees. In addition, the only luxury he had access to, was watching a movie at a nearby cinema once a week. It used to cost around 9 annas with the student discount, but his choice was quite unusual for others. He used to enjoy watching English films, and found a peculiar solace in the works of Greta Garbo, Jeanette MacDonald, and Robert Taylor were among his favourite actors and actresses. Their performances left a lasting impression on him, and provided a semblance of luxury in an otherwise quotidian life.

He completed his Master's degree in English Literature from the University of Allahabad in 1938, and was awarded a gold medal for finishing first in the university.

The day Kao received the gold medal was a moment of great accomplishment for him. It was the culmination of years of hard work and dedication, and it validated his decision to continue his studies despite facing financial constraints. Two years before completing his Master's degree, Kao's mother advised him to take up any job because the money his father had left was running out, and it was becoming increasingly difficult for Kao to continue studying. But, he knew the importance of education, and decided to pursue his Master's degree anyway. When he stood on the dais with the gold medal hanging around his neck, he felt a sense of accomplishment, knowing that he had overcome significant challenges to deserve this recognition.

However, Kao knew that he had to find work quickly because he and his mother only had 500 rupees left, which was not enough to sustain them for very long. Fortunately enough, Kao didn't have to wait long to find employment.

Kao's academic achievements and his subsequent employment with the Indian Police are testament to his unwavering commitment to his education and his country. He understood the value of education and the role it played in shaping the future of India. He, thus, dedicated his life to serving his nation and improving its intelligence capabilities. Even in his later years, Kao remained a strong advocate of education, and believed that it was the key to unlocking India's potential as a global power.

During his time at the University, Kao had the opportunity to meet with many leaders, including Jawaharlal Nehru, the first Prime Minister of India. Kao recalled being impressed by Nehru's persona and the radiance on his face, which he believed was indicative of his importance.

It was a particularly trying time for Nehru when Kao first met him. Nehru had just returned from Europe following the death of his wife, Kamala Nehru, in 1936. Despite his personal loss, Nehru continued to be a dedicated leader and played an instrumental role in shaping India's future.

Kao was heavily involved in student politics during his time at the University, and was particularly interested in issues related to student rights. He was passionate about being involved in politics, but never aspired to be a leader. Instead, he preferred to remain one step away from the limelight.

During this time, Kao also became aware of communal politics, and understood its roots in India. He vividly remembered an incident involving the INC flag, which caused a major controversy among students. While some were in favour of the INC flag being flown over the hostel, others, particularly the Muslim community, were opposing it. They argued that either there should be no flag or the flag of the Muslim League should be flown. Kao vehemently opposed this view, stating that the INC flag represented everyone in India, while the Muslim League flag only represented Muslims.

In 1939, Kao completed his first year of law school at the University, and at the age of 21, he was ready to take the next step forward into his future. He joined the Indian Police Services (IPS), marking the beginning of his illustrious career in intelligence.

❑

Initial Assignments

In 1939, R.N. Kao passed the written exam for the Indian Police (IP), and was called for an interview. During the interview, he faced a panel of distinguished individuals, which included the Chairman, an Englishman, and 2 or3 Indian members. One of the Indian members on the panel was Khan Bahadur Mohammad Zakki, a retired government advocate from Gorakhpur.

It was an important moment for R.N. Kao, as passing the written exam was only the first step towards realizing his dream of serving his country. The interview would determine whether or not he was suitable for the position, and he knew that he had to impress the panel to secure his place.

As he entered the interview room, Kao was greeted by the panel, and he nervously took his seat. As the interview began, the panel asked him a series of questions, ranging from his personal background, to his views on law and order. Despite the pressure he was under, Kao answered each question with clarity and confidence, impressing the panel with his knowledge and commitment to the cause.

As the interview drew to a close, Kao felt a sense of relief and accomplishment. He had done his best, and he knew that he had left a positive impression on the panel. It was now up to them to decide his fate, and he could only hope that they saw in him the potential he knew he possessed.

After the interview, Kao eagerly waited for the results of the Indian Police recruitment process. His hard work and dedication had paid off during the interview, but he knew that his fate was ultimately in the hands of the panel.

Finally, in March 1940, the results were declared. To Kao's surprise, he had managed to secure a place in the Indian Police. Looking back, he felt that he had gotten in purely by luck, as the circumstances had worked in his favour.

Initially, the recruitment process in UP was supposed to select only two candidates, but due to the Second World War that was raging on, there were not enough recruits available in India. As a result, they had to take in one more candidate, and that candidate turned out to be R.N. Kao.

When Kao's family heard the news of his acceptance into the Indian Police, they were overjoyed. His mother, in particular, had pinned all her hopes on Kao, and was thrilled to hear of his success. Even his younger brother was ecstatic, as this was the first time since the passing of their father that the family had experienced such happiness.

R.N. Kao's childhood was marked by his mother's strict routine and discipline. Every morning, she would wake him up before dawn and make him recite his lessons before he was allowed to eat breakfast. Then, she would send him off to school with strict instructions to study hard and excel in his studies. At the time, Kao resented his mother's strictness, but as he grew older, he began to appreciate the lessons she had taught him. Her discipline had taught him the value of hard work and perseverance, and he realized that he owed much of his success to her.

Kao's mother was his biggest supporter and cheerleader. Whenever he faced challenges, she was there to offer words of encouragement and support. Her unwavering faith in him had given Kao the strength and determination to pursue his dreams, even when life was tough.

As Kao's family celebrated his achievement, he couldn't help but feel a sense of gratitude towards them. He knew that without their love and support, he would not have been able to achieve what he had. And so, he promised himself that he would work hard to make them proud, and repay their faith in him.

Kao loved his brother, Shyam Sunder Nath Kao, a lot. He was six years younger than him. When he was born, Kao thought that his mother's love would get divided between the two, but that never happened, and Kao noticed that as he grew older, he became a good friend of his brother, and their bond became inseparable.

R.N. Kao's relationship with his brother was more than just a sibling bond—it was a connection built on love, trust, and unwavering support. When Kao received news that his brother had been admitted to the ICU of Ram Manohar Lohia hospital in January 2002, and was fighting for his life, he was filled with an overwhelming sense of hopelessness.

As the days passed and his brother's condition remained critical, Kao felt his world unravelling. He struggled to find meaning in his life as he watched his beloved brother fight for every breath, feeling powerless and desperate.

In a selfless act of love, Kao decided to get himself admitted to the same hospital, determined to remain close to his brother at all times. He wanted to be there for his brother, to offer him comfort and support, to hold his hand through every moment of pain and uncertainty.

He felt so helpless during those days that he died on January 20, 2002, just a few days before his younger brother joined him in the afterlife.

Coming back to the story of R.N. Kao and his recruitment to IP, he was excited to purchase the uniform, mess kit and other amenities required during his training period as an IP probationer.

As he embarked on his journey to the Police Training College in Moradabad, he couldn't help but feel a sense of excitement building inside him. It wasn't just the prospect of a new beginning, but also the opportunity to purchase a uniform befitting his new profession. He knew that this uniform would not only be a symbol of his identity as a police officer, but also a reflection of his commitment to duty and discipline.

So, Kao made his way to Anderson and Company in Lucknow, a first-class tailor renowned for its impeccable craftsmanship. As he browsed through the various materials and designs, he felt a sense of awe and admiration for the artistry and attention to detail that went into creating each piece.

Finally, he settled on a dinner jacket, and it was like nothing he had ever seen before—the material was beautiful, the stitching precise, and the fit perfect. He couldn't wait to wear it and show it off to his peers and superiors.

But the jacket was only part of the uniform. Kao also needed riding boots and polo boots; so he made his way to a skilled shoemaker. For Kao, this experience was more than just purchasing a uniform—it was a reminder of the beauty and luxury that life had to offer, a glimpse into a world of first-class tailors and skilled craftsmen. It was like slightly tasting the finer things in life, and he cherished every moment of it.

On April 7th, 1940, R.N. Kao reported for duty at the Police Training College in Moradabad. As he arrived, he was impressed by the magnificent officers' mess, which had been built during the First World War. The grandeur of the building was something that

Kao had never experienced before, and he couldn't help but feel a sense of pride and privilege to be able to stay there. Kao was assigned a large room with an attached bathroom.

Kao was a learned individual. He had a deep appreciation for the works of authors such as, Milton, Shelley, and Shakespeare, and he was under the impression that the world that lay in wait for him would be a reflection of how he had been brought up in his surroundings. However, the reality was quite different. When he arrived at the Police Academy, the very first thing that came to his attention was that the British officers were exceedingly impolite to the Indian students and frequently used slang. He judged them to be semi-literate and ineligible for any of the tasks they were given. It took him quite some time to adjust to the academy life.

The principal of the academy was known to have many informants around the campus, making it difficult for the officers to have private conversations without the fear of being monitored. One day, during a discussion about the Indian National Movement, the principal suddenly took an interest and directed the officers to seek Kao's opinion as he was known to be an avid reader of the Hindustan Times, a newspaper that was widely seen as a supporter of the Indian freedom movement at the time.

Kao was surprised by the principal's sudden interest and realized that the principal had been keeping an eye on him and his reading habits. He understood that he had to be cautious of his words and actions around the academy from that moment on, as he did not want to draw any unwanted attention from the authorities.

In those days, the British expected Indians to read newspapers, like the Statesman or the Republic, which were more aligned with their views, but Kao's choice of reading material made him stand out. This incident taught Kao the importance of discretion and the need to be aware of the surveillance around him.

Kao often had a feeling of being under surveillance in the Police academy, being an Indian himself. He found it uncomfortable how British officers looked down upon Indian food, often making unpleasant comments like, "Does it taste as bad as it looks?" Despite such incidents, Kao did not speak up much about it.

One of the most memorable moments for Kao during his time at the academy was when he acquired a horse within a week of his arrival in Moradabad. He loved horse riding, and it became one of his favourite pastimes. It was a great way for him to unwind and relieve the stress of his daily routine. However, it was not just a leisure activity for him; he also saw it as a skill that could come in handy in his future career in the police force. He spent hours perfecting his horse riding technique and caring for his horse. Kao cherished his love for horse riding even after leaving the police academy, and kept the horse he acquired in Moradabad for seven years. However, as time passed, the cost of maintaining the horse became a burden for Kao, and he had to let it go.

Aside from horse riding, another memorable experience at the academy was the occasional invitation from the Nawabs to visit the neighbouring town of Rampur, located about 80 miles away from their station. The Nawabs treated the officers with elegance and generosity, which was something cherished by everyone. Private shows were even screened for the officers, providing them with a much-needed break from their rigorous training.

Kao remembered one such show when he watched "Gone with the Wind", and was completely captivated by the actors and the story. The experience of being treated with such kindness by the Nawabs and getting to watch a movie was something that left a lasting impression on Kao. It was a welcome change from the strict routine of the academy and a reminder that there was still some joy and beauty in the world, even in the midst of training for a career in law enforcement.

Kao's time at the Police Academy was not the most pleasant experience due to the discriminatory attitude of the British towards Indians. However, things took a turn for the better when his training ended in 1940 and he was posted to Khiri, the headquarters of Lakhimpur Khiri district after undergoing practical district training until 1941. This change of scenery brought some relief to Kao, and he felt much better about his situation. Over the next seven years, Kao was posted to several districts in the United Provinces and gained valuable experience in his profession. Despite the challenges he faced, Kao continued to work hard and strive for success in his career.

After spending nearly seven years in various districts in the United Provinces, Kao's career took a turn in 1947 when he was deputed to the Directorate of Intelligence Bureau. This was a significant move for Kao, as it marked his entry into the world of intelligence and espionage. It was a challenging assignment, but Kao was excited about the opportunity to serve his country in a new capacity.

The Intelligence Bureau (IB) was indeed initially established by the British colonial government as a secret service agency in India in 1920. It was modelled on the lines of the British MI5, and was primarily used to counter and suppress the Indian freedom movement. The IB kept tabs on various politicians, activists, and freedom fighters, and collected intelligence about their activities.

However, after India's independence in 1947, the role and functions of the IB underwent significant changes. It was now responsible for providing intelligence and analysis to the Indian government on a wide range of issues, including external and internal security, counter-terrorism, counter-intelligence, and border management. The IB became an integral part of India's national security apparatus and played a crucial role in safeguarding the country's interests.

One of the IB's major strengths was its expertise in collecting and analyzing cross-border information. Given India's complex security environment, with multiple hostile neighbours and ongoing territorial disputes, this was a critical function. The IB's intelligence-gathering capabilities were put to the test many times over the years, and it was able to provide timely and actionable intelligence to the government, helping to prevent terrorist attacks and other threats to national security.

R.N. Kao, a dedicated employee, was recruited into India's Intelligence Bureau (IB) where he closely worked with Bhola Nath Mullik, the deputy of T.G. Sanjeevi Pillai, the first IB director from 1947 to 1950. Due to Kao's excellent work ethic and commitment, he quickly became Mullik's favourite employee. When Mullik became the director of IB after Pillai, he appointed Kao as the head of the Prime Minister's security detail, which provided Kao with the opportunity to be in close proximity to India's longest-serving Prime Minister, Jawaharlal Nehru.

Nehru and Kao developed a strong relationship, as demonstrated by Nehru's decision to appoint Kao to investigate the crash of Air India's Kashmir Princess aircraft in 1955, despite Kao's limited experience in such matters. Despite being only 37 years old at the time, Kao's proximity to Nehru and his trust in Kao's capabilities made him a clear choice for the investigation.

The Kashmir Princess, also called Air India Flight 300, was an Air India flight on a chartered Lockheed L-749A Constellation that ended in tragedy. On April 11, 1955, a bomb went off near the plane as it flew from Bombay, India, to Jakarta, Indonesia. This caused the plane to crash into the South China Sea. Only three of the 19 people on the plane made it out alive. The other 16 died. The explosion was a planned attempt to kill Chinese Prime Minister Zhou Enlai, who was supposed to be on the plane. But he missed the flight because of an illness or, as some historians say because he knew about the attack before it happened.

After the event, the Chinese government asked for a thorough investigation, which the Hong Kong government was told to do. Investigators came to the conclusion that the bombing had been done by the Kuomintang (KMT). The KMT was the ruling political party in Taiwan, and the Chinese government thought that the party was trying to stop peace talks between China and India.

As part of his investigation into the Kashmir Princess bombing, R.N. Kao had the opportunity to meet with numerous high-ranking officials from around the world. Even after the investigation was completed, Kao continued to travel abroad with Prime Minister Nehru, and used every opportunity to learn from others. This allowed him to gain valuable experience in the field of intelligence gathering and analysis.

Kao's experience and knowledge gained during his travels were invaluable when he went on to establish the Research and Analysis Wing (RAW). His ability to absorb information and learn from others was a hallmark of his career, and allowed him to establish RAW as a leading intelligence agency in the region.

❑

The Kashmir Princess

The Kashmir Princess investigation was a pivotal moment in the life of R.N. Kao. This assignment exposed him to Southeast Asia, a region that fascinated him. During this time, Kao had the opportunity to interact with delegates and important figures from around five countries within a span of just six months. This unique experience allowed him to learn a great deal about the political and cultural landscape of Southeast Asia.

Kao's involvement in the Kashmir Princess investigation was not only significant because of the exposure it offered him, but also because of the valuable lessons he learned during the investigation. This experience was a turning point for Kao, as he was able to gain insight into the complexities of international relations and the delicate balance of power in the region. He was able to witness firsthand the intricate workings of diplomacy and the challenges of conducting investigations in a foreign land.

The Kashmir Princess case was not only important due to the involvement of multiple countries, but also because of the nature of the incident. The aircraft was of Indian origin, the crew was Chinese, and it had taken off from Hong Kong before crashing into Indonesian waters. The fact that it was an attack on the Chinese premier raised serious concerns among Indian authorities, as it suggested that someone was deliberately attempting to harm the relationship between India and China.

Soon after the accident, the Chinese government made a public announcement on radio, attributing the incident to sabotage. They accused KMT (Kuomintang) agents for being responsible for the crime.

Given the gravity of the situation, the Director of the Intelligence Bureau (IB), Bhola Bath Mullik, handpicked R.N. Kao for the investigation as soon as approval was granted by Prime Minister Jawaharlal Nehru. Kao was well-suited for this role, given his extensive experience in intelligence gathering and his ability to navigate complex geopolitical situations.

Kao wasted no time and immediately set out for the investigation, taking a flight from Delhi to Bombay on April 20, 1955. He was fully aware of the importance of this investigation and the potential consequences of his findings. Kao's thoroughness, attention to detail, and analytical skills were critical to the success of this investigation.

After arriving in Bombay, Kao wasted no time in assembling his team for the investigation. He carefully selected his team members based on their loyalty, integrity and expertise. He chose Chandra Pal Singh, the Deputy Central Intelligence Officer, and Vishwanathan, an engineer from the Hindustan Aircraft Factory.

Despite being free to choose a bigger team, Kao kept his team small to ensure effective communication and quick decision-making. Within the first two days of arriving in Bombay, Kao conducted thorough interviews with the three survivors of the crash, as well as the district and operations managers of Air India in Hong Kong.

Kao's meticulous investigation yielded critical information about the individuals who had access to the aircraft before the flight, as well as the luggage that was loaded onto the plane. He discovered that no special protection had been given to the delegates who were travelling on the aircraft.

Armed with this crucial information, Kao left for Singapore on April 23 to continue his investigation. His expertise in intelligence gathering and his attention to detail would prove invaluable, as he continued to unravel the complexities of the Kashmir Princess case.

Kao had a brief stopover at the Singapore airport, where he held a few meetings before proceeding to Bandung. There, he joined a high-level meeting attended by three important leaders—Nehru, Sukarno, and Zhou Enlai—to discuss the outcome of a significant investigation.

Upon seeing R.N. Kao in Bandung, Nehru immediately took charge and provided him with instructions on how to proceed. Kao had been tasked with explaining the findings of the investigation to Chinese Premier Zhou Enlai in a private meeting. Given the sensitivity of the matter and the high stakes involved, Nehru wanted to ensure that Kao was well-prepared and knew exactly what to say.

The meeting itself was of great importance, as it involved leaders from India, Indonesia, and China. The discussions revolved around the investigation and its potential impact on the political landscape of the region. With so much at stake, it was essential that Kao's presentation to Zhou Enlai was delivered with precision and clarity.

Kao's meeting with Zhou Enlai was a pivotal moment in his life. Not only did he get to learn about Chinese traditions and how the country responds on the world stage, but he also had the opportunity to share critical information about a devastating incident that had occurred. During the meeting, Kao briefed Zhou about the bomb that destroyed the plane, and the information he had gathered through interviews with the survivors.

However, the meeting was not without its moments of unease. Kao's fountain pen leaked ink on his hand, causing him to become nervous and look for a clean paper to rub it off. It was at this point that Zhou unexpectedly got up and fetched a wet towel for Kao to clean his hand. This act of kindness and generosity left a lasting impression on Kao.

After the meeting, Zhou returned to China and gave an interview with a journalist, where he mentioned that he had never seen anyone as proud as Nehru. This statement was a revelation for Kao, as it helped him understand the intricacies of world politics, and how leaders interact with one another. It also highlighted the importance of perception, and how one's actions can impact their reputation on the world stage.

The day following his meeting with Chinese Premier Zhou Enlai, R.N. Kao left for Jakarta, Indonesia, where he recounted the details of the meeting to Prime Minister Nehru. However, despite instructions from his superior, Mullik, to return to Singapore, Nehru advised Kao to travel to Hong Kong instead.

The decision to travel to Hong Kong was not an easy one, as there were no direct flights available at such short notice. As a result, many arrangements had to be made by the embassy, which proved to be quite challenging for everyone involved. Despite the obstacles, Kao and his team were determined to reach Hong Kong.

The journey itself was a difficult one, but the team persevered and eventually made it to Hong Kong. This was an important move, as Hong Kong was a crucial hub for intelligence gathering, and was strategically located in the heart of Asia.

After arriving in Hong Kong, Kao was stationed at the Miramar Hotel for the next six months. During this time, he continued his work in intelligence gathering and analysis, focusing on issues related to China and the surrounding regions.

However, Kao soon realized that he needed to move to Peking, China, to conduct further investigations. This was a cumbersome task, as the weather and connectivity posed significant challenges. Nevertheless, Kao was undeterred and determined to complete his mission. He worked tirelessly to make the necessary arrangements, coordinating with local authorities and leveraging his network of contacts to overcome any obstacles that arose.

Upon reaching Peking, Kao met with Chinese Premier Zhou Enlai, who shared some stunning insider information with him about the bombing incident. Zhou revealed that the bomb that destroyed the aircraft was given by the United States, came from Taiwan, and was planted in the plane by agents of the Kuomintang (KMT). He even had the names of those who were responsible for the act.

Zhou proposed that they share this information with the Hong Kong Police, but with a caveat that the information should not reach the United States at any cost. Moreover, Zhou warned Kao that his own life was in danger in Hong Kong, and advised him to be careful. Kao replied that he couldn't do much to save his life, being a foreigner in Hong Kong and surrounded by Chinese everywhere. He suggested that Zhou inform the Hong Kong government about the threat to his life, if they really wanted to protect him.

Zhou acted quickly and notified the Hong Kong authorities of the danger to Kao's life. As a result, Kao noticed a significant increase in his security measures when he returned to Hong Kong. Despite the increased security, Kao remained skeptical of everything around him, knowing that the KMT could do anything to execute him.

Despite the increased security measures, Kao continued to receive warnings from the Chinese authorities about the threat to his safety. They believed that the KMT was determined to assassinate him at any cost, as his investigation was heading towards exposing some powerful individuals involved in the bombing incident.

While Kao initially felt the danger, he soon became accustomed to the situation. As an experienced intelligence officer, he knew that danger was an occupational hazard, and he had to be vigilant at all times. He continued with his investigation, collecting evidence and analyzing information that could help solve the case.

Kao's dedication to his investigation was unwavering, and he took every precaution to ensure the safety of the crucial documents he carried with him. These papers contained sensitive information that could make or break the case, and therefore he never let them out of his sight. He carried them in a briefcase everywhere he went, even during meetings and evening parties. In fact, he kept the briefcase with him even during his bathroom breaks, as he could not afford to leave it unattended.

As a seasoned intelligence officer, Kao knew that the information he carried was highly valuable, and he had to ensure that it did not fall into the wrong hands. He took extra care to keep the briefcase secure and would often keep it below his mattress while he slept. It was a testament to his commitment to the investigation.

Kao's friends and colleagues soon became aware of the importance of the briefcase to him, and started referring to it as his "darling".

RN Kao was well-aware that the Kashmir Princess investigation was not just a matter of intelligence gathering and detective work. He had to navigate complex political relationships with multiple countries involved in the case, including China, Britain, and Hong Kong. Additionally, as an agent of the Indian government, Kao had to be politically correct at all times to avoid any diplomatic incidents that could have far-reaching consequences.

Moreover, Nehru's reputation was at stake, and Kao knew that he had to deliver results, while also ensuring that the investigation did not damage India's relationships with other countries. Thus, he had to be extremely careful about his actions and words while investigating the case.

However, the challenges did not end there. From the beginning of the investigation, K.M. Raha, the Deputy Director-General of the Civil Aviation Department, was not happy with Kao's involvement in the case. Raha felt that he should have been given more importance in the investigation, since he held a senior position in the department. This created tension and competition between Kao and Raha, adding another layer of complexity to the investigation.

Moreover, Kao's favour with Nehru further added to the resentment towards him among his colleagues. Despite these internal challenges, Kao remained focused on the task at hand and continued to work diligently to uncover the truth behind the Kashmir Princess case.

On his return to Hong Kong from Peking on 18 May 1955, Kao gave a list of suspects to the Governor, and suggested that they take immediate action to apprehend them. He knew that capturing the suspects would be crucial to gaining the confidence of the Chinese government, who had been vocal about their suspicion that KMT agents were responsible for the sabotage of the Kashmir Princess.

In addition to his meetings with the Governor, Kao also met with his British counterparts to update them on the progress of the investigation. He was careful to balance his communication with both parties and ensure that his actions did not harm India's relationships with either of them.

Throughout the investigation, Kao remained mindful of Nehru's instructions that nothing should be done that could damage India's relationships with any of the countries involved. He worked diligently to ensure that the investigation was conducted with utmost professionalism, diplomacy, and impartiality.

It was true that during the investigation of the Kashmir Princess case, Kao became aware that both China and Britain had their own agendas and were using India for their own purposes. Kao realized that India was chosen for the investigation because both China and Britain believed that India could be easily influenced and manipulated to serve their interests.

However, Kao did not let this knowledge affect his work on the investigation. He remained focused on gathering evidence and identifying the perpetrators of the attack. He was committed to upholding the integrity and reputation of the Indian intelligence agency.

It was also true that the Chinese Premier was very interested in the Kashmir Princess investigation and was closely following the progress of the case. As mentioned, the Chinese Premier was in frequent contact with Kao, and wanted to be kept informed about the investigation in order to maintain China's confidence in India's handling of the case.

However, it was also possible that the Chinese Premier's interest in the investigation was motivated by political considerations. The attack on the Kashmir Princess had been a major embarrassment for the Chinese government, and they may have seen the investigation as an opportunity to demonstrate their commitment to rooting out anti-Chinese elements.

Kao was in for a shock when he learned that the prime suspect in the Kashmir Princess bombing case, Chou Chu, had already fled the city six hours before Kao handed over the list of suspects to the Hong Kong Police. This news left Kao suspicious of everyone around him, and he couldn't help but feel that he was being manipulated by all parties involved in the case.

Despite this setback, the Hong Kong Police continued to urge Kao to obtain more information from the Chinese authorities so that they could make arrests. However, the Chinese only provided information in bits and pieces, and at inconvenient times such as late at night or early in the morning. This left Kao feeling frustrated and powerless. Nevertheless, he remained patient and persistent in his pursuit of the truth.

This turn of events showed Kao that the investigation was not going to be a straightforward one. It was clear that there were powerful forces at play, and that he would have to navigate the political landscape very carefully. The pressure was mounting, but Kao was determined to stay focused and determined in his pursuit of justice.

Following the investigation, the British authorities became convinced that the Kashmir Princess had been sabotaged. However, they were not pleased with the way the Chinese were handling the matter. They felt that the Chinese were not providing all the information they had in a timely manner. The British authorities were hoping for more support and cooperation from the Chinese in order to apprehend the suspects and bring them to justice. The lack of cooperation from the Chinese and the suspicion that they were hiding something only added to the frustration and tension in the investigation.

At the end of May 1955, Chinese Premier Zhou Enlai arrived in Hong Kong and met with the Governor to discuss the progress of the investigation. He appreciated the work done by Kao and even wrote a letter to Nehru expressing his appreciation for Kao's efforts. However, Zhou was still not convinced by the work of the Hong Kong police and the British authorities. He felt that they were not doing enough to cooperate with the investigation, and were not taking the matter seriously.

Krishna Menon, the leader of the Indian delegation in the UN and considered second-in-command to Nehru, suggested that Mullik should visit Hong Kong to demonstrate India's seriousness in the investigation. Hence, in June 1955, Mullik arrived in Hong Kong.

Mullik, being a high-ranking official in India's Intelligence Bureau was sent to Hong Kong to assist Kao in the investigation, and to show India's strong commitment to resolving the case.

Mullik's involvement in the case proved to be a game-changer, as he brought a fresh perspective and energy to the investigation. He was successful in holding separate meetings with both the Chinese and British officials and keeping them happy by following the policy of Pandit Nehru. Although the British were genuinely trying to solve the case, the Chinese were not satisfied with their efforts as they believed that the British were being secretive about the KMT espionage network, and were only focusing on the crashed plane.

Mullik was also briefed by Kao about his investigation and was impressed with the effort that Kao had put in so far. Mullik played the role of a mediator between both parties, and was able to maintain a cordial relationship between them. His diplomatic skills were commendable as he managed to balance the interests of both the Chinese and British officials.

After Mullik returned to India, Zhou wrote a letter of complaint to Nehru, accusing Mullik of showing partiality towards the British in the investigation. Nehru, upon receiving the letter, carefully assessed the situation and realized that Zhou's accusations were based on a misunderstanding of the facts. Nehru promptly wrote back to Zhou, reassuring him that Mullik, along with all other Indian officials, was unbiased and committed to finding the truth behind the crash. Nehru's response highlighted the importance of impartiality in the investigation and emphasized India's commitment to carrying out a thorough and transparent investigation, free from any political bias or pressure.

Nehru's response to Zhou's complaint demonstrated India's stance on maintaining an objective and impartial approach to the investigation, despite the political tensions between China, Taiwan, and the UK. Nehru's assurance helped to build trust and credibility with both the Chinese and the British in the investigation, ensuring that both parties felt their interests were being taken into account.

After the investigation into the Air India plane crash had been going on for some time, the Hong Kong government decided to offer a reward of 100,000 Hong Kong dollars to anyone who could provide information about the incident and those responsible. Despite the potential monetary gain, no one seemed to come forward with any new information or leads.

❑

The Learning

By the middle of June 1955, it had become evident that one of Kao's primary objectives had been achieved—to prove that the plane had crashed due to sabotage, and not due to any mechanical failure. This was further confirmed by the Indonesian report on the investigation, which revealed that there was clear evidence of sabotage on board.

Kao's relentless investigation and determination had paid off, and the truth about the cause of the crash had been established. This finding was significant as it disproved the initial speculation that the crash was a mere accident, and it highlighted the presence of a larger conspiracy.

The confirmation of sabotage on the aircraft raised several questions about the motives behind the act, the identities of the individuals involved, and the potential ramifications of such an attack.

Despite establishing that the plane crash was a result of sabotage, the investigation was still far from uncovering the complete truth behind the incident. The two most pressing questions, who was responsible and why they did it, remained unanswered. Unfortunately, progress on this front was being impeded by the ongoing Cold War tensions between the Chinese and the British.

Initially, Hsiung provided Kao with a great deal of valuable information during their first few meetings. However, his cooperation soon became limited and he started to withhold important details. The British authorities were doing everything in their power to assist in the investigation, but the lack of cooperation from the Chinese was making it increasingly difficult to make any significant progress.

After the initial information from Hsiung, Kao and the Hong Kong police conducted extensive investigations and made several arrests in Hong Kong. They discovered a large network of KMT secret intelligence agents operating in the city, but connecting this network to the plane crash was proving to be a challenging task. The KMT agents were highly skilled and well-trained in espionage tactics, and they were extremely cautious about leaving behind any evidence that could implicate them in the sabotage. Also, the main accused of the plane crash, Chou Chu was still on the run.

The situation between the Chinese and the Hong Kong police became increasingly tense, as the Chinese officials accused some Hong Kong police officers of being involved with the KMT. As a result, the Hong Kong police became more determined to uncover the truth behind the plane crash on their own and requested that the Chinese officials leave.

Meanwhile, Hsiung had been cooperating with Kao in the early stages of the investigation and providing valuable information. However, he later demanded that Kao hand over recorded documents of the investigation that the British had shared with him. The British, however, refused to share any information with the Chinese officials. This brought the investigation to a standstill and left Kao at a dead end.

Now the question for Kao was—what good was he doing while staying in Hong Kong when both governments were refusing to work in cooperation with each other? Kao was confused about how to proceed and had no idea what he should do next.

Despite the tensions between the Hong Kong police and the Chinese officials, Kao managed to maintain his connections with some of the top officials, and was able to gather crucial information about the investigation. He discovered that Chou Chu's roommate had come forward with information about the events leading up to the crash, following the announcement of the reward by the Hong Kong government. According to the roommate's testimony, Chou Chu had confided in him about the plan to sabotage the plane. He had taken heroin and revealed that he had met with KMT agents who had given him the bomb. Chou Chu had then slipped the bomb into the cavity above the right wheel of the plane while cleaning it.

Furthermore, the roommate also revealed that after the crash, Chou Chu had gone to the KMT agents to claim his reward, but they had refused to pay him anything because Zhou Enlai was not on the plane. This information suggested that the KMT agents had planned to kill Zhou Enlai on various occasions before. He also told that their plan was to assassinate Kuo Mu Ju, who was coming to India as the head of the Chinese delegates for the conference; but when they got to know about the Zhou Enlai trip to Bandung via Hong Kong, the plan was changed.

Despite the fact that Kao had made progress in uncovering the truth behind the plane crash, he found himself facing two significant obstacles. The Chinese government was unhappy that the Hong Kong police were unable to prosecute Chou Chu, who was believed to be responsible for the bombing of the plane, while the British authorities in Hong Kong were putting pressure on Kao to leave the city as soon as possible. Kao was aware that he had to leave Hong Kong, so he informed the Indian authorities about his situation. However, the Indian Ministry of External Affairs refused his plea to leave Hong Kong, and instead advised him to continue his investigation.

The Indian authorities' decision was motivated by their desire to maintain a good relationship with the Chinese government. They did not want to give the impression that India was withdrawing its cooperation with China in investigating the crash. However, this decision put Kao in a difficult position. He was being forced to stay in Hong Kong, where his presence was no longer welcome, and he was unable to make any further progress in the investigation.

Throughout the month of July 1955, Kao found himself being tossed back and forth between the governments involved in the investigation, with little to no progress being made. Kao had no choice but to stay in Hong Kong, as he had no other options available to him. He felt like a mere puppet, with no one truly cooperating with him.

Kao attempted to seek further assistance from the governor, but his requests were denied, with no additional data being shared with him. It became increasingly apparent that the case had become nothing more than a political game for all involved, and Kao was simply there to bear witness, with little opportunity to actively participate in the investigation.

In the midst of the political turmoil surrounding the investigation, there was further development that only served to deepen the divide between the British and the Indians. In July of 1955, Indian Prime Minister Pandit Nehru publicly acknowledged the Chinese government's contribution to the investigation, which infuriated the British officials in Hong Kong. They argued that it was the British who had provided the majority of the resources and manpower for the investigation, and that Nehru should have acknowledged their efforts instead of those of the Chinese.

However, Kao, who was caught in the middle of the dispute, pointed out that the Chinese did play a role in the investigation by providing information about the suspects to the Hong Kong police. He further argued that the Indian government was not wrong in acknowledging the Chinese support.

Kao began to realize that the British authorities in Hong Kong were only concerned with maintaining a positive image for themselves rather than actually helping with the investigation. Despite Kao's requests for assistance, they were reluctant to share any new information with him. However, everything changed when Zhou Enlai summoned Kao to Beijing, and he was instructed to be there by 20 August. Suddenly, the British and Hong Kong authorities started to cooperate with Kao once again. They wanted to be seen as supportive of his investigation, and thus, improve their image in the eyes of China. In fact, they even shared some information with Kao that had previously been kept hidden from him.

The responsibility of deciding what to report to the Chinese fell on the Indian authorities in Delhi. They had to decide whether Kao should report the information he received from the British and Hong Kong police, or express his own feelings about the case. In the third week of August, clear instructions were given to Kao on what to report. He was instructed to only report the information he had received from the Hong Kong police and not to disclose any additional information to the Chinese authorities.

This decision by the Indian authorities was likely influenced by political considerations. India was trying to maintain a delicate balance between China and Britain, and disclosing sensitive information could have jeopardized this balance. It is also possible that the Indian authorities did not want to reveal the extent of their intelligence capabilities to the Chinese.

Regardless of the reasons, Kao followed the instructions and reported only the information he received from the Hong Kong police to the Chinese authorities.

Kao left for Beijing on 25 August 1955 under immense pressure. The British officials had attempted to persuade Kao by revealing the name of the main culprit, who was a KMT agent known as Wu. Finally, on the 27 August, Kao met Zhou Enlai, and the meeting lasted for three hours. Although much time was wasted during translation, one thing was clear: Enlai was not convinced that the British officials were doing their best to catch the main culprit of the crime. This put Kao in an uncomfortable position as he was expected to report only what he had received from the Hong Kong police and British officials.

During a conversation, Zhou Enlai posed a question to Kao about his personal opinions regarding an ongoing investigation. Kao took some time to gather his thoughts and provided only factual information. He also mentioned that the Hong Kong police might soon submit their report to the Chinese government. Zhou expressed skepticism about this, stating that he didn't think the Hong Kong police would share the investigation's findings. However, Kao reassured Zhou, based on his personal experience over a long period, he believed it would be impossible for the Hong Kong police to remain silent for long.

Kao was aware of the political pressure from Enlai, but he also knew that he had to remain neutral and not say anything that could be used for political gain. Despite Enlai's attempts to sway him, Kao remained steadfast and true to his principles. When Enlai expressed his skepticism about the efforts of the British and Hong Kong authorities to catch the main culprit of the crime, Kao responded diplomatically. He acknowledged that he too was initially disheartened by the slow progress, but he had witnessed the authorities doing their job fairly well. Kao was careful not to give any information that could be misconstrued or used to manipulate the situation for political gain.

Zhou Enlai's insistence on the alleged involvement of two Hong Kong police officers with KMT agents put Kao in a difficult position. Kao, being an intelligence officer, understood that making accusations without evidence could harm the credibility of the investigation. Therefore, he responded cautiously and said that he was not aware of any such thing, and would not comment on any unproven allegations.

Kao's response was important in maintaining the integrity of the investigation, and it also showed his commitment to the principles of justice and fairness. Zhou Enlai's attempt to politicize the investigation by making unfounded allegations against the Hong Kong police officers was a cause for concern, but Kao did not let it affect his professionalism.

Enlai's furious comment put Kao in an uneasy position. On one hand, he was being accused of being deceived by the Hong Kong government, and on the other hand, he had to maintain his neutrality as an investigator. Kao understood that Enlai was trying to manipulate him to gain political mileage, but he remained silent and composed during the outburst. Kao's silence showed his professionalism and his commitment to the truth. He did not want to indulge in any kind of political maneuvering or speculation.

As the meeting between R.N. Kao and Zhou Enlai went on, Kao started to feel like he was losing his integrity in front of the Chinese Premier. However, things took an unexpected turn when the next day, Enlai extended a special invitation to Kao for dinner at his summer palace located outside Beijing. This was a significant honour for Kao, who was a relatively junior officer in the Indian intelligence agency.

At the dinner, Enlai expressed his appreciation for Kao's diligent efforts and hard work in the investigation. Kao was relieved and felt that his integrity had been restored in the eyes of the Chinese government.

As Kao returned to Hong Kong, he briefed the governor about his meetings in Beijing, and told them about whatever happened in Beijing. By the end of the investigation, Kao received a lot of information about KMT agents, but he never mentioned where he got the information.

In his investigation, Kao discovered that the Kuomintang (KMT) intelligence organization, known as the Fifth Liaison group, was operating in Hong Kong under the guise of an electrical shop located somewhere on Temple Street. The organization's main objective was to arrange the travel of KMT agents into China, and safely extract them when they encountered problems. The owner of the shop, Kwan Tsau Kee, was only minimally connected to the KMT's activities, but the other two workers were key members.

In March 1955, the KMT agents met Wu, who came in contact with the Fifth Liaison group. They asked Wu if he knew of anyone who worked at the airport and could assist them. After a few days of searching, they found a man named Chou Chu, and several meetings were held in various locations to plan and build trust. Initially, Chou Chu refused to assist them out of fear for his life, but after some persuasion and the promise of a reward of 600,000 Hong Kong dollars, he changed his mind.

Chou Chu underwent several training sessions in which he was taught how to handle and use a time bomb. The training was conducted by the KMT intelligence organization, the Fifth Liaison Group, in Hong Kong. Finally, Chou Chu was handed a time bomb in a brown paper bag by a person named Wong at the Movieland Hotel. He was then instructed to plant the bomb on the plane that was carrying the delegation of Chinese diplomats to the Bandung Conference in Indonesia.

On April 10, 1955, Chou Chu successfully planted the bomb on the plane which exploded mid-air, causing the tragic crash of the Kashmir Princess. The explosion killed 11 people, including five members of the Chinese delegation.

Despite his significant contribution to the sabotage, Chou Chu was not paid the promised sum. This caused frustration and fear in him, leading him to flee the country in a cargo plane to Taiwan about a month after the attack.

After conducting a thorough investigation, Kao was able to uncover the identity of Wu, the handler of large sums of money that fueled the KMT's operations in Hong Kong. Wu's real name was Wu Yinchin, and he was originally from Shanghai, but had been living in Hong Kong for the past two years. With this information in hand, Kao and his team continued their pursuit of Wu and Chou Chu, the man responsible for planting the bomb on the Kashmir Princess.

Despite gathering a significant amount of information, the Hong Kong police were unable to apprehend either Wu or Chou Chu, leaving Kao frustrated with the lack of progress in the case. Even after his return to India, Kao was kept in the loop about the investigation's developments, which ultimately seemed to be leading nowhere.

The inability to bring those responsible to justice only added to the tragedy of the Kashmir Princess incident, leaving Kao and his team to wonder what more they could have done to prevent it from happening.

Towards the end of his notes, Kao recounted an incident where he had been invited for an evening tea session with the then Prime Minister of India, Jawaharlal Nehru. During the course of their conversation, Kao had briefed Nehru on various aspects of the case, and Nehru had listened attentively without uttering a word. At the end of the conversation, Kao expressed his admiration for the way Zhou Enlai had treated him and other officials. Kao had been impressed by the Chinese officials' courtesy and hospitality, and he had conveyed this sentiment to Nehru.

In response to Kao's remark, Nehru had smiled and made a comment about the Chinese being "very polite and charming when they want to." At that time, Kao had not fully grasped the meaning behind Nehru's words. However, as events unfolded during the 1962 war between India and China, Kao came to understand the underlying implication of Nehru's statement.

In total, R.N. Kao spent around six months on the investigation of the Kashmir Princess, and during this investigation, he learned many things about world diplomacy. The first thing that he learned was that anything that appears to be crystal clear is always a mirage. Kao's investigation of the Kashmir Princess also revealed the complex web of international relations, and the extent to which countries go to protect their interests, even if it means sacrificing innocent lives. This experience gave him a deeper understanding of the world of espionage and diplomacy. This investigation may have resulted in no proper conclusion, but it was still the first step in the realization of Kao's dream and ambition. He learned that the world of espionage and diplomacy is not always black and white, and that sometimes, the lines between good and bad can be blurred. Despite the lack of a proper conclusion, this investigation fueled Kao's determination to pursue his dream of becoming a spy. This mission led to a gain various contacts, and he used every bit of them in later years. Kao's persistence and resourcefulness paid off as he eventually founded the top intelligence agency, RAW. His experience from the investigation proved to be invaluable in his career, which was waiting eagerly for him to arrive.

❑

The Skill to Observe and Learn

Kao had time to learn in Hong Kong and China while investigating the Kashmir Princess. As he writes about it in his reports, there was one more thing that was quite amazing about him and that was his observation skills. He had observed the people living in Hong Kong and in China, and how their lives showcased the contrast in the living standards of both the areas and their population.

Kao's experience in Hong Kong was quite challenging. When he arrived in Hong Kong in late April, he quickly discovered that the city was experiencing a water scarcity. This meant that running water was only available for a few hours each day, making it difficult for him to carry out his daily routine. On top of that, he found that he did not have appropriate clothing for the warm and humid Hong Kong climate.

As soon as he got settled in Hong Kong, he made it his first priority to draw his travel allowance and visit a tailor. He ordered two suits for himself which would be more suitable for the climate.

Kao's observations of Hong Kong's social dynamics are insightful. He noted that the city was home to a mix of Chinese and Indian people, who had distinct cultural differences despite being from the same continent. There was a clear gap between these two communities, which were often segregated from one another. This cultural divide had an impact on many aspects of daily life in Hong Kong, including the food people ate, the languages they spoke, and the customs they practiced.

Furthermore, Kao observed that there was also a stark divide between the rich and poor in Hong Kong. This divide was especially noticeable among the Indian community, where there were clear differences between the Sindhi businessmen who were prosperous, and the Sikhs from Punjab who were mostly working for the Hong Kong police or doing odd jobs in hotels, shops, and other establishments. This division within the Indian community was indicative of broader socioeconomic disparities in Hong Kong.

Kao's observations highlight the complex social dynamics of Hong Kong, a city that was undergoing significant changes during his time there.

Kao had a mixed experience while living in Hong Kong. On one hand, he found the Sindhi community's habit of wearing kohl in their eyes and speaking English with an accent quite annoying. However, he appreciated their hospitality, and found them to be friendly and helpful during his six-month tenure in Hong Kong.

On the other hand, Kao found Hong Kong to be an interesting place, despite not appearing so on the surface. Hong Kong was a wealthy city where money could buy anything and everything. The locals loved to flaunt their wealth through their attire and homes. However, upon entering China, Kao noticed a stark contrast. The locals may look the same, but the flashy displays of wealth he saw in Hong Kong were nowhere to be found. Instead, he saw people with blank expressions on their faces. Everyone dressed in the same manner and sometimes in the same colour as well. China was a fascinating country in that sense.

The women of Hong Kong were renowned for their impeccable sense of style, which frequently exceeded that of their European contemporaries. They were well-groomed, confident, and stood tall. The women of Hong Kong were very proud of their appearance, and it was evident in the way they carried themselves. Every element was carefully planned and expertly executed, from their stylish shoes and accessories to their exquisitely tailored dresses. Regardless of whether they were in the office or out on the town, they knew how to dress to impress, and make a statement.

Furthermore, their self-assurance extended beyond just their sense of style. Women from Hong Kong were renowned for being independent and strong-willed. They were confident and poised, in addition to being ambitious and career-driven.

Compared to Hong Kong, there was a notable difference in the way women lived and dressed in mainland China. Although they continued to dress elegantly, they had a very different outlook on beauty and fashion than their Hong Kong counterparts. Women in mainland China placed a greater emphasis on simplicity and functionality than their counterparts in Hong Kong, who often adorned themselves with fashionable accessories. They were dressed elegantly, but without ornate details or ostentatious embellishments. Instead, they chose simple, modest clothing that was both practical for their daily activities and comfortable.

Kao's observations about mainland China, specifically Beijing, shed light on the challenges faced by the younger generation in the country. The city was overpopulated, and the younger generation struggled to find suitable living arrangements, which made it difficult for them to get married and start a family. The housing problem was evident, with most houses being single-storey structures, except for a few newly-built government buildings.

Despite these obstacles, Kao was impressed with the city's infrastructure. The roads were wide and impeccably clean, with not a single piece of trash in sight. The city was also undergoing rapid construction, which held the promise of better things to come in the future.

However, Kao noticed that despite the city's progress, the people did not seem very happy. The challenges of daily life, coupled with the lack of personal space and living arrangements, had taken a toll on people's well-being. The younger generation, in particular, seemed to be struggling with the prospects of their future.

Kao's observations on transportation in mainland China brought to light the stark disparity between officials' and commoners' access to private vehicles. The majority of the streets were deserted because only big officers and officials could afford and own cars. In contrast, the average person mostly relied on walking or riding a bicycle to get around the sizable city. The officials who owned cars had access to luxurious limousines with curtains on their windows to shield them from the common people's view. This division between the officials and the general public was a reflection of the social division that was then present in mainland China. The general public had limited access to buses for public transportation. This served to emphasize even more how few resources are available to the general public in comparison to the privileges enjoyed by the officials.

As R.N. Kao was Zhou Enlai's personal guest, he provided him with a car and two interpreters who accompanied him on all of his city tours. He was enjoying the perks of being an important person in the city. Chinese used to take Kao on lavish meals, opera performances, and other historic tours, which included trips to see the Great Wall of China, in order to keep him amused and away from the city's everyday problems.

Kao's notes also include some interesting observations about Chinese opera shows. He was informed that every character in the show could be distinguished by observing their attire. Each character, whether it was the villain or hero, had a specific dress and hairstyle that set them apart. Kao was also surprised to learn that in traditional Chinese opera shows, women's parts were played by men.

In fact, Kao found it amusing to learn that in his younger days, Zhou Enlai, had also played the role of a woman in some traditional opera shows. This observation highlights the cultural significance of Chinese opera shows, and the willingness of performers to take on different roles regardless of gender.

However, Kao's notes also reveal his personal opinion on Chinese music. He found it too loud and considered it a cheap imitation of Western music.

He also cherished the fact that Zhou Enlai always catered the dinners to the preferences of the host. V.K. Menon, Nehru's confidante, visited Beijing at the same time as Kao. And Enlai had set up dinner in his honour. Kao found it amusing that Menon's entire menu was kept vegetarian, as he was a vegetarian. This demonstrated how respectful the Chinese were of the host country's cultural preferences.

Kao noticed that when the Chinese want to please someone, they extend incredible hospitality. The whole menu was designed in favour of Menon. Everything was vegetarian, but was shaped like a chicken, fish, and other non-vegetarian items. Kao admitted that the food lying in front of them didn't feel appetizing at all, but the lengths to which the Chinese had gone to please Menon were extraordinary.

Kao, throughout his tenure in Hong Kong and China, silently observed the everyday lives of people and was thankful for the privilege he got to study and work simultaneously during the investigation.

❑

The Next Assignment: Ghana Calling

During the Commonwealth Games in London, India's Prime Minister Jawaharlal Nehru met with the newly independent country of Ghana's Prime Minister Dr. Kwame Nkrumah P.C. During this meeting, Dr. Nkrumah made a request to Nehru that would lead to Kao's next assignment in Ghana. The request was simple: Ghana wanted to form an intelligence unit and sought India's assistance in doing so.

Interestingly, the request for India's assistance had been informally brought up the day prior by the secretary of Ghana's Prime Minister to Mullik, who was the Director of the Intelligence Bureau (IB) at the time.

India and Ghana had a strong relationship, and India was willing to assist Ghana in any way possible, as long as there was no conflict of interest. The discussions between the two countries regarding the request for assistance with intelligence training went on for several months, and eventually, Ghana's Prime Minister sent a letter outlining their requirements. The letter stated that Ghana would be sending two officers to India for training, and one of them would become the lead of Ghana's intelligence service. In addition, Ghana requested that one of India's intelligence officers accompany them to Ghana for a year to help establish the groundwork for their intelligence service, and recruit suitable officers for the position.

Various meetings were held in India to discuss the best approach to fulfill Ghana's request, with high-ranking officials from external affairs and ministers involved in the discussions. It was important for India to maintain a positive relationship with Ghana, as they were both members of the Commonwealth. India never wanted to turn down any requests for assistance, especially when it came to helping other countries establish important services, such as intelligence services. India's goal was to befriend and establish relationships with as many countries as possible, and this request from Ghana provided an opportunity to strengthen the bond between the two nations.

Finally, when the framework of response was ready, Pandit Nehru was briefed on what the other officials felt and the response for Ghana was drafted. Pandit Nehru wrote back to Dr. Nkrumah in November 1957,accepting the request and showing their eagerness to help Ghana in their endeavour to establish an intelligence unit of their own, as they were ready to help in every way possible. This was the beginning of the long-term relationship with Ghana, and Nehru was proud of it. Nehru's letter had a detailed plan of what they could expect from India, and how things would be revealed in stages. It was all prepared by Mullik and his team cautiously ascertaining that would be no problem in the future.

The letter proposed a three-stage plan to establish an intelligence agency in Ghana. The first stage suggested that the director of IB visit Ghana to conduct a thorough examination of the situation on the ground. This visit would aid in determining the appropriate course of action for the Indian officials. This stage would last for 2–3 weeks. During this stage, the Indian officials would closely examine the situation and gather all necessary information to make an informed decision. It was crucial for them to take their time and thoroughly assess the situation before deciding on a course of action.

The second stage involved training two officers from Ghana's intelligence agency in India alongside the Indian intelligence agency. This stage would run concurrently with the first stage. The aim of this stage was to enhance the capacity of Ghana's intelligence agency by sharing knowledge and expertise with their Indian counterparts.

Finally, in the third and final stage, a senior officer from the Indian intelligence agency would accompany the Ghanaian officers, who had been trained in India, back to Ghana to help establish their own organization. This three-stage program was designed to strengthen the intelligence capabilities of Ghana and foster a collaborative relationship between the two countries in the field of intelligence gathering and analysis. The program also aimed to promote regional security and stability by building the capacity of Ghana's intelligence agency.

This 3 stage program would help Ghana set up its intelligence infrastructure, and also ensure that it was functioning efficiently. This collaboration between India and Ghana highlights the importance of international cooperation in building strong intelligence networks. It also demonstrates India's commitment to supporting other countries in their efforts to enhance their national security.

It was necessary for the Indian counterpart who would be chosen to go to Ghana to realize that he was only going as an advisor and not the head of the department; so it was necessary for the Ghana government to first choose the leader for their team, and then, the third stage will commence.

This shows that India was willing to provide guidance and expertise to other nations without imposing its own leadership. The approach taken by India in this situation reflects a respectful and collaborative approach to international relations.

At that time Kao was working as a chief to the security of Pandit Nehru. He was selected by Mullik for the task to go to Ghana, and was relieved from his current duty to protect the PM of India. Kao accepted the offer and went to Ghana where he worked as an advisor to the government.

The British were reportedly unhappy with Ghana's decision to ask India for help in setting up an intelligence agency in the nation, though they did not publicly express their displeasure. They may have felt betrayed by Ghana's decision to seek assistance from India instead of them because they were used to controlling the affairs of their former colonies. They did, however, exhibit a strong desire to participate in the entire scenario. It is possible that they were looking for a way to interfere and continue to exert some influence over Ghana's intelligence operations.

The initial phase of the plan, which called for the director of IB to travel to Ghana to assess the situation there, ran into problems and was ultimately scrapped. The plan's second phase, which involved training two Ghanaian officers in India, was still moving along according to schedule.

Paul Yankey, the Superintendent of Police, and Ben Forjoe, the Deputy Superintendent of Police, travelled to India in April 1958 to take part in an intelligence agency training program. While they were in India, the two officers were to receive training from Kao, an IB officer.

Another IB officer, H.J. Kriplani, was chosen to work with Kao as an assistant in order to make sure the training was successful. The two officers from Ghana received training in a variety of areas related to gathering, analyzing, and managing intelligence. That included training on various information gathering and analysis methods, as well as management and leadership techniques for an intelligence agency.

Kao's observations about the two Ghanaian officers who received training in India are interesting. According to him, both officers were from similar backgrounds and had similar levels of education. Although their English language skills were not advanced, they were both fluent in English and able to express themselves reasonably well.

However, during the initial days of training, the officers' Ghanaian accents did present a barrier to communication. The Indian trainers were not accustomed to the Ghanaian accent, which made it difficult for them to understand what the officers were saying. Nonetheless, over time, the officers were able to overcome this barrier and establish a more effective mode of communication with their Indian trainers.

Kao noted that the officers were aware of the importance of the task they had been chosen for, and were eager to learn as much as they could during their time in India. Despite their limited language skills, they were able to grasp the basics of intelligence gathering and analysis that were being taught to them.

Kao and his team had a well-thought-out plan to ensure that the two Ghanaian officers felt comfortable and at home during their stay in India. They recognized that, in order to effectively impart knowledge and skills, it was important to first establish a good rapport and sense of friendship with the officers.

Rather than focusing solely on theoretical knowledge, the Indian trainers made a conscious effort to create a friendly and welcoming environment for the two officers.

By doing so, the trainers were able to build a sense of trust and camaraderie with the officers. This made it easier for the officers to ask questions, seek clarification, and generally engage more deeply with the training. The officers felt more comfortable sharing their own knowledge and experiences with the trainers, which resulted to be more helpful for the trainers to better understand the context and challenges of intelligence gathering in Ghana.

Kao's observations about the two Ghanaian officers provide some interesting insights into their personalities and working styles. Despite coming from similar backgrounds, Yankey and Forjoe had very different personalities. Yankey was outgoing, friendly, and always ready to crack a joke, but was also clever and skilled at his work. On the other hand, Forjoe was more serious and focused, always keeping his mind on the task at hand.

While these personality differences may have made for some interesting dynamics during the training period, Kao notes that both officers were instrumental in helping him during his subsequent visit to Ghana. The rapport and relationship that Kao had built with the officers during their time in India continued to flourish when Kao arrived in Ghana, and the officers were able to provide valuable insights into the local context and challenges.

The bureaucratic hurdles faced by Kao demonstrate that even the most well-planned and thought-out proposals can be held up by logistical and administrative concerns. Despite being the only name put forward for the position, Kao's deployment to Ghana was delayed by discussions surrounding his salary and perks.

The issue of compensation is a thorny one in any international collaboration, and it is not surprising that this was a major point of contention in Kao's case. Given his rank and experience, it was understandable that he would expect to be compensated at a level commensurate with his expertise and responsibilities.

However, as Kao's proposed salary would have exceeded that of the head of the Indian high commission in Ghana, it is also understandable that there would be concerns about setting a precedent or creating diplomatic tension by paying a foreign national more than a government official of a similar rank.

During the bureaucratic negotiations over Kao's deployment to Ghana, a news article from the Tribune newspaper created a stir and prompted an immediate investigation. The article claimed that the Ghanaian government had formed a committee to seek assistance from the UK, Canada, and Pakistan in setting up an intelligence agency in Ghana. The Indian government had no knowledge of this development and launched a thorough investigation into the matter. The investigation ultimately revealed that the report of the committee seeking help from Pakistan was false, but it turned out that there was indeed a committee established by the Ghanaian Prime Minister to oversee the intelligence agency's formation. Despite spending several years in Ghana, Kao was not privy to the details of this committee's operations. Nonetheless, the revelation did not impede Kao's work, and he chose to ignore it.

It was a tough time for Kao when the issue of his salary and allowances was being debated in the Indian bureaucracy. He was losing interest in the whole scenario and even told Mullik on multiple occasions to drop his name from the proposal. The constant discussions about his remuneration were making him feel embarrassed.

Despite this, Kao was a patriotic Indian who wanted to see his country gain something out of the whole exercise. Mullik convinced him that it would be a great disappointment for the country if he did not accept the offer, so he reluctantly accepted the compromise that was made. Although he was not happy with the decision, he decided to put the interests of the nation above his own personal interests.

Before Kao could leave for Accra in Ghana, there were a few more complications that needed to be dealt with. The Ghanaian government wanted Kao to spend two years in Ghana to train their officers and establish the intelligence unit, but Mullik was not ready to allow Kao to be away for that long. He could only allow Kao to go for one year.

Another issue was that Kao did not want to leave his accommodation in Delhi which was 93 Lodhi Estate. However, according to Indian government rules, if he left for Ghana for more than six months, the accommodation would be given to someone else. To tackle this problem, Kao made a deal that he would go for six months, come back to Delhi on leave for a while, and then go to Ghana again as a fresh depute.

These negotiations took some time, but eventually, everything was settled, and Kao was set to leave for Ghana. After resolving the problems, the Kao couple embarked on a journey to Accra via Rome on an Air India flight, followed by a connecting flight on the British Airways.

The journey to Accra for the Kao couple turned out to be more exciting than they had anticipated. Upon reaching Rome, they were informed that the British Airways employees had gone on strike for a period of ten days, which meant that they would be stranded in Rome for the duration. Initially, Mrs. Kao was worried about the situation, fearing that their expenses would skyrocket, and they would run out of money.

However, the Indian embassy in Rome stepped in to help the Kao couple. They provided incentives to cover their expenses, and British Airways, which was responsible for the strike, covered the cost of their hotel stay. As a result, the 10-day stay in Rome became an unexpected holiday for the Kao couple.

During their stay, they had the opportunity to explore Rome and enjoy its many attractions, such as the Colosseum, the Vatican, and the Roman Forum. They also indulged in the city's famous cuisine, enjoying delicious pasta and pizza dishes, among others.

Despite the unexpected delay, the Kao couple made the most of their time in Rome. On 25 October 1958, Kao and his wife finally arrived in Accra after their unexpected 10-day stay in Rome. They were warmly welcomed at the airport by the acting foreign secretary, Mr. Grant, as the foreign minister was on leave at that time. In addition to Mr. Grant, other officials were also present to receive the couple, including the two officers Yankey and Forjoe, who were trained by Kao in India, and the second secretary of the Indian High Commission in Accra.

The warm reception by the Ghanaian officials was a good sign for Kao and his mission. It showed that the Ghanaian government was serious about establishing an intelligence unit and was willing to work closely with the Indian government. Kao was optimistic about the prospects of his mission and was ready to begin his work. But as Kao settled into his new home in Ghana, he soon discovered a major obstacle to starting his work. The two officers he had trained in India, Yankey and Forjoe, had not taken any initiative to start the intelligence work in Ghana. In fact, they had not even reported to their government about the training they had received in India. Kao found himself in a difficult situation, as he had to start everything from scratch, without even a designated office space. The lack of preparedness on the part of the Ghanaian officers was a major setback, and Kao realized that he had a daunting task ahead of him. He would need to build a new intelligence unit in Ghana, virtually from the ground up.

Kao was initially optimistic that the preparations for the establishment of the intelligence unit in Ghana would be completed soon. However, he soon discovered that despite assurances from everyone involved, there was still a lot of work to be done.

Although the two officers had assured Kao that everything would be ready soon, he soon found out that the office designated for the intelligence unit was far from being completed. Kao learned that the idea to transform a house into the headquarters of the intelligence agency had come from the Prime Minister himself, but the two officers were only able to set up a few chairs, tables, and a telephone in the office. Kao realized that he would have to take matters into his own hands to get things moving.

Kao received a list from the Prime Minister of Ghana, which included 21 people selected for the team of the new intelligence organization. The individuals' ages ranged from 21 to 49 years, and Kao was surprised to find that none of them was graduates, nor were any of them, police officers. Some even had political backgrounds. Despite his curiosity, Kao did not question the Prime Minister's choice.

He also noticed that the British intelligence officer and another British gentleman named McKay, who was in charge of the special branch in Ghana, were making special efforts to be friendly with him. Kao could not help but compare their behaviour to their approach during his investigation in Hong Kong. He observed that the British had a different approach to different people, depending on what they were looking for. Nevertheless, Kao was thankful for their assistance and was enjoying their help.

There was one more thing that Kao observed about the British officials he encountered. In West Africa, the British he met were not as competent and efficient as those he had worked with in India. He attributed this to the fact that the British viewed India as the crown jewel of their Empire, and therefore, they invested more resources and effort in maintaining their rule there. On the other hand, West Africa was regarded as a less important and less desirable region for British colonial rule, partly due to the challenging weather conditions. This lack of investment and attention from the British colonial authorities in West Africa may have led to a lower calibre of officials being sent to serve in the region, in comparison to those who were deployed to India.

Kao had a mixed opinion about McKay, the British official who was in charge of the special branch in Ghana. Despite noticing his quick temper, Kao felt that McKay was a man with a golden heart. However, Kao also felt bad for him being posted in a country like Ghana where he was not being utilized according to his calibre. McKay was under family pressure, as he had to provide for his wife and four children with no other qualification other than being in a police uniform. This led him to serve in Ghana, even though he had served in the Second World War and also in Palestine during its division. Kao noted in his journal that

McKay was of medium build and had ginger hair. He often looked like an Irishman to Kao. Kao remained in touch with him for a fairly long time. The last time they had conversed, McKay was in Swaziland in South Africa.

After spending some time in Ghana, Kao was eager to meet with the Prime Minister, Dr. Nkrumah, and discuss the progress of their mission. Finally, after a week of waiting, Kao was granted a meeting with the PM in his office. During the meeting, the first thing Kao explained to Dr. Nkrumah was Mr. Mullik's inability to visit Ghana as planned. However, Kao was quick to reassure the PM that India remained fully committed to their promises, and would continue to work towards strengthening the ties between the two nations. The meeting provided Kao with an opportunity to discuss other matters related to their mission and build a stronger relationship with the Ghanaian government.

Kao couldn't help but notice the distinct physical features of Dr. Nkrumah when he finally met him in his office. The first thing that caught Kao's attention was the Prime Minister's bright, large eyes, which seemed to radiate a sense of energy and intelligence. Kao could also see that the Prime Minister had a prominent forehead, which further added to his impressive appearance.

As he sat across the table from Dr. Nkrumah, Kao felt a sense of awe at the magnitude of responsibility the Prime Minister carried on his shoulders. Not only was he leading the nation of Ghana, but he was also seen as a figurehead for the entire continent of Africa. This sense of duty and responsibility was reflected in the way Dr. Nkrumah carried himself, with a commanding presence and a sharp, focused mind.

Despite the weight of his responsibilities, Dr. Nkrumah appeared calm and composed as he spoke with Kao. Kao could sense the Prime Minister's commitment to the development of his country and his desire to work closely with India to achieve their shared goals.

Kao had the opportunity to meet the PM of Ghana for the first time at his official residence, which was once the British governor's residence during the colonial period. The castle now served as the official residence and office of the PM.

The PM was an excellent speaker of English and his own language as well, and he had a charisma that could sway the masses through his speeches. He was also known for paying attention to his appearance, and Kao appreciated this quality since he was also someone who paid attention to his sense of styling.

During their meeting, Kao inquired about the PM of Ghana's priorities when it came to intelligence work. The PM expressed his concerns and shared them in great detail, leaving Kao with the impression that he had high expectations from both India and Kao. Kao then laid out his plans for addressing the PM's concerns and explained the steps he would take.

The PM mentioned that the British had offered their assistance, and that he was open to using it, if needed. He also asked Kao to advise on the scope of both intelligence and counter-intelligence. Kao explained that extensive training would be necessary for these tasks and that India may need to provide some assistance as well. The PM readily agreed to Kao's plan without hesitation.

As the meeting came to an end, Kao thanked the PM for his time and assured him of India's unwavering commitment to the development of Ghana's intelligence capabilities. The PM reciprocated the sentiment and expressed his confidence in Kao and his team's abilities. With a handshake, they bade farewell to each other, ready to embark on the mission to strengthen Ghana's intelligence operations.

In his first meeting with Dr. Nkrumah, Kao was impressed by his sincerity that when he left the office, he suddenly felt the burden of responsibilities that he had taken on his shoulders. It never appeared to him to counter him anywhere. But throughout his one-year stay in Ghana, Kao had felt that PM had a very frank nature when he used to talk. It was a friendly and free talk which Kao never felt like opposing.

Kao realized that managing the operations alone would not be sufficient to help Ghana establish and maintain a smooth flow with the new intelligence organization they were building. Hence, he decided to focus on further training the officers to ensure that they had the skills and knowledge required to carry out their responsibilities effectively. He encouraged officers, Yankey and Forjoe, to take charge of the operations, and train others with the same enthusiasm. Kao also taught them how to report accurately and extract information from ground zero, as well as how to approach various situations. Despite his best efforts, Kao struggled to maintain a good relationship with the local politics, which was at its peak during that time.

To make things easier for Kao, the British secretary of Dr. Nkrumah, Erika Powell, proved to be of great help. She played a significant role in smoothing things out for Kao and his team. Kao noticed that she genuinely loved the PM, and served Ghana in every possible way. Her assistance and support were invaluable in helping Kao and his team navigate the political complexities of the region. Kao was grateful for her support, and he knew that without her help, their situation in Ghana would have been much more challenging. Erika experienced a moving moment when she departed from Ghana to England due to the marriage of the Ghanaian leader to an Egyptian woman, but discussing this would be a digression.

Kao also wrote in his notes that Erika was the only reason he was able to fight the thinking of people who thought of him as an intruder in their country. The people who thought so were the Ghanaians and the British as well. Not everyone was thinking in the same manner as Kao about the whole mission. Some even thought that he would take advantage of the Ghanaians and leak out information in the making of this new intelligence unit. During this tussle, the strength came from Erika who took care of various things for Kao.

The establishment of the intelligence unit in Ghana under Kao's leadership was a remarkable achievement. With his excellent training skills, Kao kept his focus on preparing the officers and ensuring they were able to perform their duties with precision. As a result, Kao and his wife became quite famous in the state for their contribution towards building the intelligence network. However, as Kao had to take care of his house in India, he had to leave Ghana after six months. It was a small break, and after taking care of his personal matters in India, he returned to Ghana to complete his assignment.

The first year of Kao's assignment passed swiftly, and he was able to make significant progress in establishing the intelligence network in Ghana. However, as time passed, it became clear that Kao needed to be replaced by someone else as there were many other things that needed to be done in India. The responsibility of finding a suitable replacement fell on Mr. Mullik, who eventually chose Sankaran Nair to take over Kao's role.

According to Nair's book, he was not the first choice for this assignment. It was first offered to Amrit Midha. However, when Mullik approached him to take over Kao's position in Ghana, it was a sudden and unexpected decision. Nair was taken aback by the offer, and took some time to think it over.

Nair discussed the opportunity with his wife and found that she was supportive of the idea. He also sought advice from Kao himself, who urged Nair to take the offer without any delay. After careful consideration, Nair finally accepted the offer and prepared to take on the new role in Ghana.

The Nair couple landed in Ghana on December 1959 and stayed in Ghana till early 1961. Nair had big shoes to fill as Kao had made a significant impact in Ghana, and had established a strong foundation for the intelligence unit. Nair was determined to continue the good work and carry on Kao's legacy. However, he also faced some challenges in establishing a rapport with the local officials and navigating the political landscape in Ghana.

Despite the impediments, Nair worked hard and made a name for himself in Ghana. He helped the intelligence unit in Ghana to work efficiently for a long time. His experience and intelligence helped Ghana tremendously in the coming years. During his stay in Ghana, Israelis tried their best to maintain a good relationship and reach the Indian subcontinent, but Nair was stubborn about the approach and stayed away from it because he considered, it was not his business and eventually, Israelis let it go.

In February 1966, R.N. Kao and Sankaran Nair had a significant meeting with Dr. Nkrumah, the then President of Ghana, when he was visiting Peking in China via Delhi. This was the last time Kao and Nair met with him before his unfortunate ousting by a military coup. During his visit to India, Dr. Nkrumah also met with Mrs. Indira Gandhi, who was the Prime Minister of India at that time. The meeting became quite embarrassing for Indira Gandhi as Dr. Nkrumah kissed her on the cheek, a Western tradition that was not common in India at that time.

Dr. Nkrumah had always welcomed Kao and Nair with open arms, and had a very friendly and cordial relationship with them. After his meeting with them, he left for Peking, never to return to Ghana again. His presidency was cut short by a military coup that overthrew his government, and he was granted asylum by his friend in Guinea, where he finally succumbed to cancer.

With Dr. Nkrumah's overthrow, the chapter of India's intelligence assistance to Ghana came to an end. However, this chapter proved to be a crucial stepping stone for India's Research and Analysis Wing (RAW) as it gained valuable experience and expertise in providing intelligence support to foreign governments, which it continues to do to this day.

❑

Road to Becoming War Ready Nation

The war between India and China in 1962 was a watershed moment for India's information gathering efforts. Due to this, the Indian government came to the conclusion that it required specialist troops that were capable of carrying out clandestine operations beyond enemy lines and beyond the border, in particular in the Himalayan region. Because of this, the Intelligence Bureau (IB) was forced to create two new agencies to deal with the situation.

The Aviation Research Centre (ARC) was established in 1963, and R.N. Kao, who was chosen as the head of the department, headed it till 1966. It was in charge of aerial reconnaissance and surveillance, and was the first agency to be established. Intelligence gathering from the sky is accomplished through the use of a large number of aircraft and unmanned aerial vehicles (UAVs). It was made with the cooperation of India and the US aftermath of the

1962 war. The main task for the unit was to capture photographs and technical intelligence from inside the Tibet region and Xinjiang region with the help of eight C-46 aircraft and four smaller planes. They were stationed in the region which was code-named 'Oak Tree', later revealed as the area of Odisha.

The Special Frontier Force (SFF) was the second agency, and it was established in 1962 with assistance from the Central Intelligence Agency (CIA) as well as Tibetan exiles. Covert operations are the responsibility of the SFF, which is tasked with carrying them out along the border with China, especially in the Himalayan region. The members are Tibetan refugees who have received training in guerilla warfare as well as mountaineering skills.

During the military actions that took place in India during the Kargil War in 1999, these agencies were extremely important. The ARC was responsible for providing crucial intelligence regarding the positions and movements of the adversary, whereas the SFF was responsible for carrying out operations behind enemy lines, and playing a pivotal part in the capture of strategic peaks in the Kargil region.

In the midst of this crisis, on 19 November 1962, Indian Prime Minister Jawaharlal Nehru sent two SOS letters to the President of the United States, seeking assistance. It was a desperate appeal to John F, Kennedy to prevent China from capturing the northeast territory of India. The letters also emphasized the gravity of the situation, and the urgent need for American aid.

The response from the United States was prompt and significant. A high-level meeting was convened at the White House, which included the heads of the Central Intelligence Agency (CIA) along with other top officials. The objective of the meeting was to discuss the Indian crisis and explore possible solutions.

After a lengthy discussion, the attendees came to a decision. They agreed to send a small, high-level military mission to India in order to assess the situation on the ground. This mission was intended to gather intelligence on the Chinese military's strength and movements, as well as to evaluate India's capacity to defend itself.

This visit was crucial in helping the United States to understand the situation in India, and to formulate an effective response. It was also important for India, as it provided valuable intelligence and allowed for the development of a plan of action.

The US tactical team stayed in India for three days, and during that period, they tried to access the whole situation from a new angle, and took many inputs from Mullik and his team. They were trying to figure out how they should proceed but before they could do anything, China themselves declared a unilateral ceasefire. For the next six months, the US helped India in many ways.

The situation in India during the 1962 war with China was dire, with the entire Brahmaputra valley under serious attack, and massive forces from China trying to capture Assam, Tripura, Manipur, and Nagaland. The Indian army was struggling to hold its ground against the better-equipped Chinese forces, and it seemed like the situation was slipping out of control. The letter that Nehru sent to the US President was to seek help to strengthen the Indian Air Force which was not well-equipped at that time. India had no modern equipment to fight the Chinese troops. The radars were not capable enough to detect enemy movement; even the planes were not as advanced as needed to defend India's front and for that, help from the US was the need of the hour.

Despite India's bitter defeat in the 1962 war with China, the country received crucial military and logistical support from the United States, which helped to tilt the scales of the war in India's favour. This assistance from the US was instrumental in reshaping

India's military and intelligence capabilities in the aftermath of the war. The US helped India to establish new specialized and well-equipped army divisions, which would enable them to respond more effectively during future conflicts. The US also played a significant role in boosting India's arms and weapons production, which was essential in ensuring enhanced military strength, self-sufficiency and national security. Furthermore, the US provided crucial support in strengthening India's air defense through joint exercises and the provision of better fighter planes.

It is widely believed that the US provided assistance to India in strengthening its air defense not only to help India in its time of need but also to gain access to Indian equipment and intelligence to monitor China's activities and nuclear capabilities. This would have allowed the US to gather valuable intelligence on China without directly entering the region itself.

However, it is important to note that this assistance also helped India in improving its own military capabilities and preparedness, which was crucial in deterring any future aggression from China.

While the US did have strategic interests in providing this assistance to India, it was a mutually beneficial partnership that helped both countries.

During the IB-CIA joint venture, an opportunity arose for the US to gain crucial intelligence about China's nuclear program. Seeking permission from Nehru to fly U-2 missions over Tibet and Xinjiang, the US was able to gather the information that China was preparing to conduct nuclear tests in the Lop Nur region. This intelligence was shared with the US president, who was informed that China would become a nuclear power within the next few months. As predicted, China conducted its first nuclear test in October 1964, solidifying its position as a nuclear-armed state.

Meanwhile, Kao was occupied with establishing the Aviation Research Centre (ARC) from scratch. He sought and received help from the US, setting up a state-of-the-art facility, the best in all of Asia. With Kao's involvement in various missions ranging from Hong Kong to Ghana, to the Prime Minister's security, and establishing ARC, he was building his reputation within the country alongside gaining valuable experience.

❑

Learning from Failures

In the aftermath of the 1962 war with China, India realized the importance of being prepared for any future conflicts that may arise. It was a time of great uncertainty, and the Indian government understood that it would be better to invest in their military capabilities than to regret not doing so in the face of adversity. Little did they know that the sequence of wars had only just begun. Soon after the conflict with China, India found itself engaged in yet another war, this time with their neighbour Pakistan. The war lasted for 22 days, and came at the time of great turmoil in India.

The death of Jawaharlal Nehru, India's first Prime Minister, had left the country in a state of mourning and uncertainty. Pakistan, on the other hand, was backed by several superpowers, which only added to India's troubles.

The 1962 war had already taken a toll on India, both economically and politically. And with the new conflict with Pakistan, the country was struggling to make ends meet. The war came at a time when India was already grappling with several internal issues, including poverty, unemployment, and political instability.

During the war with Pakistan, the leadership of India played a crucial role in ensuring the country's success. Lal Bahadur Shastri, who had become the Prime Minister after Nehru's death, led the country with great resolve and determination. He urged the nation to "Jai Jawan Jai Kisan," which means "Hail the soldier, Hail the farmer," emphasizing the importance of both the military and the agricultural sector in building a strong and self-reliant nation.

Under Shastri's leadership, the Indian military fought bravely against Pakistan's aggression. The defense ministry, led by Y.B. Chavan, played a key role in coordinating the country's military operations. The Indian Air Force carried out several successful air strikes against Pakistan, while the army mounted a strong ground offensive.

Despite Pakistan's numerical advantage, the bravery and determination of the Indian soldiers turned the tide in India's favour. The country's armed forces made remarkable gains, capturing key territories and securing their borders. Pakistan suffered heavy losses, both in terms of personnel and equipment, and was eventually forced to surrender.

The war with Pakistan in 1965 marked a significant shift in India's approach towards national security.

Shastri recognized the importance of strong leadership in times of crisis, and he took bold steps to protect India's territorial integrity. He authorized the Indian military to launch a series of airstrikes against Pakistan, targeting key military installations and infrastructure.

The decision to go to war was not an easy one, but it was necessary to safeguard India's interests. Pakistan had been overindulgent in its activities in Kashmir, and India had to respond to protect its sovereignty. The war may have been destructive, but it was a necessary step to ensure that India's security and territorial integrity were not compromised.

However, it is important to note that the war had a devastating impact on both India and Pakistan. It led to the loss of thousands of lives and caused widespread destruction. Even today, the scars of the war continue to haunt the people of both countries.

As Gohar Ayub Khan, the son of former Pakistani President Ayub Khan, in an interview with 'Outlook' has acknowledged, the war should not have taken place. It changed the dynamics between the two countries, and created a legacy of mistrust and hostility.

Indeed, the 1965 war between India and Pakistan had far-reaching consequences, not just for the two countries, but also for the region as a whole. The war left Pakistan feeling humiliated and vulnerable, especially in its eastern wing, which is now Bangladesh.

The loss to India in the war further emboldened the Bengali population in East Pakistan, who had long been subjected to discrimination and neglect by the Pakistani establishment. East Pakistan was alarmed by the lack of protection provided by the Pakistani army during the war, which left them exposed to Indian aggression.

The Pakistani government's response to the East's demands for greater autonomy and rights was dismissive, which only further fueled the anger and frustration of East Pakistan. Sheikh Mujibur Rahman emerged as the leader of the Bengali nationalist movement, and he demanded a separate and independent country for East Pakistan.

India provided significant military and political support to the Bengali movement, and eventually, Pakistan's heavy-handed military intervention in East Pakistan triggered a full-blown war between India and Pakistan in 1971. The war resulted in the formation of Bangladesh as an independent country, with India playing a pivotal role in its creation.

The 1965 India-Pakistan war was a tumultuous period in the history of both nations, marked by several intelligence failures that exposed India's vulnerabilities in terms of intelligence gathering and analysis. One such failure was the Pakistani operation Gibraltar, which aimed to infiltrate militants into Indian-administered Kashmir. This operation was in full swing for several days, yet India's intelligence agencies were unable to detect or prevent the infiltration, leading to a chain of events that culminated in a full-scale war between the two nations.

Even after the war ended, India's intelligence agencies were unable to gain any insight into Pakistan's likely response to such a significant loss. As a result, the Indian army was caught off-guard when the Pakistani offensive was launched, leading to significant territorial gains for Pakistan. Moreover, India had no idea about the magnitude of the attack that Pakistan could launch on India. If Indian intelligence had an inkling of the advanced ammunition and equipment that Pakistan had at its disposal, supplied by the United States, it would have predicted that the war would not last more than a month. However, the war ended after just 22 days, and India was left to grapple with its intelligence failures.

Nevertheless, amidst this series of intelligence failures, one positive development for India emerged. The country realized that it needed to step up its intelligence-gathering capabilities to avoid being caught off-guard in the future. This realization led to the establishment of the Research and Analysis Wing (RAW), India's external intelligence agency, which marked a significant shift in India's intelligence operations. RAW was established with the primary objective of gathering intelligence on external threats, and supporting India's national security interests.

The establishment of RAW (Research and Analysis Wing) was a significant milestone in the history of Indian intelligence. With the failures of the intelligence agencies during the 1965 war, the need for a dedicated external intelligence agency was felt more than ever before. It was Indira Gandhi's foresight and leadership that led to the establishment of RAW in 1968, with R.N. Kao as its first Chief.

R.N. Kao, who had previously headed ARC (Aviation Research Centre), played a critical role in setting up RAW from scratch. He was known for his impeccable leadership skills and his ability to think outside the box. He was also the head of the external affairs division of IB, during the same time as when he was the head of ARC, and that gave him a deep understanding of India's external security challenges.

The political scenario in India was also changing rapidly during this period. Lal Bahadur Shastri's sudden death created a leadership vacuum in the country, and Indira Gandhi, who was considered a weak leader at the time, emerged as the new Prime Minister. She faced stiff opposition from within her own party because being the daughter of Jawahar Lal Nehru, she was believed to have got the office in inheritance, but she proved to be a shrewd politician who knew how to get things done. She made several bold decisions, including nationalizing banks and abolishing privy purses, which earned her the admiration of the masses.

Indira Gandhi's success was also due to the team she had assembled around her. P.N. Haksar, who was appointed as her secretary in 1967, was one of the most influential members of her team. He was a Kashmiri Pandit who had never lived in Kashmir. He was a brilliant strategist who played a key role in shaping India's foreign policy during the 1970s. Haksar and Kao worked closely together to establish RAW and ensure its success.

Despite various speculations about the establishment of the Research and Analysis Wing (RAW), there is no official document that provides a clear justification for its creation. R.N. Kao, the founder of RAW, does not mention its reason in his notes. However, according to Sankaran Nair, a close friend of Kao and an intelligence expert, RAW was formed as a solution to the conflict between the Indian Army and Intelligence during the 1965 Indo-Pakistan war.

During the conflict, the military accused intelligence of being a total failure, and demanded the creation of a military intelligence unit to operate in foreign territories. However, not everyone in the bureaucracy favoured this idea. When Indira Gandhi became the Prime Minister in 1966, she faced the challenge of ending this conflict. She relied on the expertise of R.N. Kao, who, in just one month, presented her with a complete structure for an organization that could handle espionage on foreign land. Cabinet Secretary D.S. Joshi suggested the name "Research and Analysis Wing" to keep it under covers.

Indira Gandhi was very particular about the recruitment process for RAW. She expressed her belief that the wing should not only recruit officers from the Indian Administrative Service (IAS) and Indian Police Service (IPS), but also consider officers from the street if necessary. According to her, officers with street smarts were needed to carry out espionage activities in foreign lands, as they would often work alone and face unpredictable situations.

The idea behind the establishment of RAW was very clear: it should not be bound by the usual structure of bureaucracy, but should work extraordinarily in extraordinary situations. And to ensure these things, the head of RAW had to be a resourceful and intelligent person, because he was answerable for many things.

Indira Gandhi entrusted R.N. Kao with the task of handpicking his team for the newly-established RAW. Kao immediately reached out to his close friend and former colleague, Sankaran Nair, who had succeeded him in the Ghana assignment. Nair was delighted to receive the invitation from Kao to discuss the new development over lunch.

During their conversation, Kao shared the details of the new department being structured under Mrs. Gandhi's instruction, and proposed that Nair join in. Kao also mentioned that Nair was denied a promotion by the new boss of IB, for which Kao was apologetic. However, he assured Nair that he would do his best to get him the recognition he deserved.

Nair didn't hesitate to accept the offer, even though it meant sacrificing his promotion. For him, the opportunity to work with a close friend and contributing for the country was more important. Kao and Nair's teamwork was crucial in the early days of RAW, and it helped lay the foundation for the organization's success.

The formation of RAW and its separation from the IB caused jealousy and intolerance among the IB officials who had considered foreign intelligence as their prized possession. Additionally, the Ministry of External Affairs (MEA) was also unhappy with the formation of RAW, which created friction between the departments. Initially, Kao tried to handle the situation on his own, but when he became frustrated, he approached Haksar and expressed his concern that he would not be able to work effectively, if he did not have independence from the usual bureaucratic ways.

Haksar recognized the validity of Kao's concerns and advised Mrs. Gandhi to take action. She took the matter seriously and wrote a letter to the Cabinet Secretary, highlighting the need for RAW to have a certain level of autonomy and independence from the bureaucracy. This step was crucial in ensuring that RAW could operate effectively and efficiently, without being bogged down by bureaucratic obstacles.

The problems for RAW were still not getting resolved. Although the support of Haksar and Mrs. Gandhi's backing helped considerably during many things for the department, but still things were getting delayed on many fronts. Nair wrote in his book that petty things like furniture, office building, and account staff were getting delayed because of the intervention of IB.

Everything was taken care of by Nair and meanwhile, Kao was looking to expand the working of RAW in other countries. He wanted 13 stations to be formed in 13 different countries. Foreign Secretary T.N. Kaul took the demand seriously, but reduced the number to 8 stations.

Kao had a specific reason for each of the eight stations that he wanted RAW to establish a base in. These reasons were carefully thought-out and strategically planned to gather valuable intelligence for the security of India.

The first two stations that Kao targeted were Paris and Bonn. During those years, this region had become a hub for the production and distribution of sophisticated weapons to various countries in Asia and Africa. Pakistan was one such country that was acquiring weapons, including Mirage aircraft, to strengthen its air force. This posed a direct threat to India's security, and Kao recognized the importance of monitoring these activities closely.

Moreover, Paris and Bonn were also known for their technical knowledge of rocketry and aerodynamics, which China was using to gain an advantage in its military capabilities. Kao understood the need to keep a close watch on these developments as they could impact India's strategic interests.

Thus, Kao's decision to establish a base in Paris and Bonn was based on the need to gather insider information about Pakistan and China's activities in the region. This information would be invaluable to India's national security, and Kao was determined to ensure that RAW had a presence in this area to gather intelligence and protect India's interests.

Kao identified Istanbul as another station for RAW due to its strategic importance as a hub of international relations. During World War II, Istanbul played a key role in mediating and facilitating communication between various countries. As such, it became a hotbed for espionage activities. Furthermore, Pakistan had a significant interest in Istanbul as it provided training to its personnel. Thus, to keep a close eye on Pakistan's activities and gather crucial intelligence, it was imperative for RAW to establish a station in Istanbul. By doing so, RAW would be able to monitor the training of Pakistani personnel and gather valuable intelligence about their activities in the region. Additionally, Istanbul's location made it a perfect base for operations in the Middle East, the Balkans, and Central Asia.

Hanoi and Phnom Penh were chosen by Kao as stations for RAW because they were becoming hotspots for Chinese interventions. The Chinese government was increasing its involvement in the political affairs of these regions, and it was crucial for India to keep a close eye on these activities. The Indian government needed to understand China's policies and changing political scenarios in these areas to formulate effective strategies for India's own interests. Hence, having a RAW station in these regions would enable India to gather crucial intelligence about Chinese interventions, which would be crucial for India's national security.

Mauritius was strategically important as it regained its importance as a key location in the Indian Ocean after the closure of the Suez Canal. It provided a crucial point for monitoring sea traffic in the region, and gathering intelligence on potential threats to India's maritime security.

Fiji, on the other hand, was strategically located in the Pacific Ocean, making it an important station for gathering intelligence regarding the activities in the region. This was especially important given the increasing involvement of global powers in the Pacific and India's growing interest in the region.

Trinidad, located in the Caribbean Sea, was important for monitoring sea traffic in the region and gathering intelligence on potential threats to India's maritime security. Additionally, Trinidad provided a key location for gathering intelligence on drug trafficking and other illicit activities that could pose a threat to India's interests.

Overall, these three stations were carefully selected by Kao to ensure that RAW had a presence in key locations across the globe, allowing India to monitor potential threats and safeguard its interests both regionally and globally.

Despite facing several obstacles from various departments, Kao remained resolute in his efforts to establish the RAW, and create a strong intelligence network for India. He was well-aware of the importance of his work and knew how to navigate the bureaucratic hurdles in his path.

His efforts eventually paid off, and the RAW proved to be a valuable asset for India, particularly during the 1971 East Pakistan crisis. Kao's foresight and strategic planning ensured that India was well-prepared to deal with any threats to its security, and RAW played a crucial role in providing the intelligence needed for India's successful military campaign.

❑

RAW and Eastern Pakistan

In the mid- and late 1960s, the world was undergoing a period of significant change and unrest. In France, student protests and labour strikes were sweeping the country, with young people calling for greater freedoms and an end to the authoritarianism of the state. In the United States, the civil rights movement was at its peak, with African-Americans fighting for equal rights and an end to segregation. Meanwhile, in East Pakistan (now Bangladesh), the Bengali-speaking population was rising up against the West Pakistan-dominated government, demanding greater autonomy.

Amidst all this turmoil, India was also experiencing its own set of challenges. The country was still reeling from the aftermath of the partition and the creation of Pakistan, which had left deep scars in the psyche of the nation. The economy was struggling, and the country was facing food shortages and high inflation. In this context, it was crucial for India to have a robust intelligence network that could keep an eye on both internal and external threats.

Sheikh Mujibur Rahman was not only the founder of the language movement, but also the leader of the Awami League, a political party in East Pakistan that aimed for greater autonomy and eventually independence. In the 1970 general election, the Awami League won a clear majority in the National Assembly of Pakistan, but the ruling military junta led by General Yahya Khan refused to transfer power to the democratically elected government. This led to massive protests and civil disobedience in East Pakistan.

Meanwhile, in West Pakistan, specifically Lahore and Karachi, there were also protests against the government due to basic shortcomings, such as food shortages and inflation. Marshall Ayub Khan, who had previously ruled Pakistan for over a decade with the support of the military, was losing control of the situation.

In this context, Zulfikar Ali Bhutto emerged as a major player in Pakistani politics. He was a former foreign minister and had broken away from the Ayub Khan regime to form his own political party, the Pakistan People's Party (PPP). Bhutto positioned himself as a champion of the people's rights and was seen as a viable alternative to the military-backed regime. However, his rise to power would also have significant consequences for the future of Pakistan.

It became increasingly evident that more than twenty years after the formation of Pakistan, the East and West regions had little in common other than their shared religion. The cultural differences between the two wings of the country were profound, and the idea of Pakistan as a religious state was not beneficial for East Pakistan. Instead, many Bengali-speaking people in the East felt disconnected and unrepresented in the political system, which was dominated by the West. The central government in Islamabad was seen as out-of-touch and unsympathetic to the needs of the East. The language barrier between the two parts of Pakistan was becoming a huge difference and East Pakistan was asking for a solution to it. This growing sense of alienation and frustration led to increased demands for greater autonomy and eventually independence.

The population difference between East and West Pakistan became a significant factor in their relationship. According to the census of 1961, East Pakistan had a larger population of 50.84 million compared to West Pakistan's population of 42.9 million. However, this population difference was not reflected in the political representation of the country as a whole, which frustrated the people of East Pakistan even more. The dominance of West Pakistan in political affairs and its focus on Arab culture rather than the Eastern part of its own land made the situation worse. The cultural and linguistic differences between the two regions also contributed to the growing sense of estrangement and vexation among the people of East Pakistan. The formation of Pakistan on the basis of religion alone was not enough to hold the two regions together when there were such significant differences in language, culture, and political representation.

Sheikh Mujibur Rahman also referred to as 'Bangabandhu', was a significant player in East Pakistani politics. He was born in the village of Tungipara in modern-day Bangladesh around 1920. He was raised in a low-income home and received his education in Calcutta, India. He joined the Muslim League, the biggest political party in British India, after completing his schooling.

Sheikh Mujibur Rahman was a fervent advocate of Pakistan and thought that in order to protect the interests of the Muslims in the area, a distinct Muslim state needed to be established. He was disappointed with how the West Pakistani elite were treating East Pakistan, even though when India and Pakistan had split apart.

Rahman started calling for more autonomy for East Pakistan at the beginning of the 1960s. He believed that the ruling class in West Pakistan was more concerned with preserving their own privilege and power than they were with the needs of the people of East Pakistan. He felt that the people of East Pakistan should have more influence over the political and economic decisions that the nation makes.

Midway through the 1950s, Sheikh Mujibur Rahman founded the Awami League, a new political party that replaced the Muslim League. The party was devoted to the objective of giving East Pakistan more autonomy. He was not thinking about the further partition of Pakistan until early 1960, but the second Kashmir war that happened between India and Pakistan in 1965, changed Mujibur's thoughts about the further partition of Pakistan.

In 1965, President Ayub Khan, who was leading Pakistan at that time, believed that they had the upper hand on India, and decided to initiate a war over the Kashmir issue. However, this decision proved to be a foolish one, as the war quickly escalated and both sides suffered losses. As the war dragged on, the western front of Pakistan received much of the attention and resources, leaving the eastern part of the country defenseless. It was only due to sheer luck that the war ended before it could have taken an even uglier turn.

The war made the people of East Pakistan realize that they were vulnerable and exposed to external threats without proper defense and support from West Pakistan. They started questioning their status and representation in the country. They felt neglected and ignored by the government in the West, which was more interested in their own agendas and interests. This led to harbouring resentment towards the West Pakistani rulers among the Bengali-speaking population in the East. As questions and concerns began to arise from East Pakistan regarding their security and protection, President Ayub and the military were unable to provide a convincing answer. Their response was that China would come to their rescue if India decided to attack the eastern borders of Pakistan. However, this answer was not reassuring to the people of East Pakistan, as it was unclear if China was actually capable or willing to provide military support in the event of a conflict. The lack of a concrete plan or solution from the government further eroded the trust and confidence of East Pakistan in the central authorities. The feeling of neglect and abandonment grew stronger.

The aftermath of the war had severe consequences for Pakistan. Mujibur Rahman and his party, the Awami League, took up the cause of East Pakistan's autonomy and started political agitation. They demanded that East Pakistan be given greater political representation and economic development. This political agitation gained momentum, and Pakistan suffered from continued unrest and instability.

Ayub Khan's credibility suffered a major blow, and he was forced to resign in 1969. General Yahya Khan then took over as the new president of Pakistan. However, the unrest in East Pakistan continued to escalate, and the Awami League emerged as the dominant political force in the region.

In an effort to address the grievances of East Pakistan, Yahya Khan announced the general elections in 1970. However, the elections became a turning point in the history of Pakistan.

On December 7, 1970, General Yahya Khan finally announced the elections that had been postponed once earlier. However, Sheikh Mujibur Rahman had certain demands to be met before the elections, but Yahya Khan showed no interest in them. Despite his doubts, Mujibur prepared for the elections, knowing that they may not solve the issues in East Pakistan.

Just a month before the elections, a devastating cyclone hit East Pakistan, killing around one million people. India stepped in to help as a goodwill gesture, providing 50 million rupees and sending essential supplies on trucks to aid the victims. The volunteers of the Awami League also played a significant role in the relief efforts. However, West Pakistan failed to respond to the disaster, causing further agitation among the Bengalis.

The lack of assistance from West Pakistan highlighted the growing divide between the two regions, with East Pakistan feeling neglected and unimportant to the central government.

The results of the 1970 elections came as a surprise to many, as it was difficult to predict which party would win. Bhutto's Pakistan People's Party (PPP) and Mujibur's Awami League of East Pakistan were both popular in their respective regions. However, when the results were announced, it became clear that the Awami League had a sweeping victory in East Pakistan, winning 167 out of 169 seats. In contrast, the PPP won only 83 out of 144 seats in the western part of the country. This also meant that the Awami League would rule the whole of Pakistan because out of 313 total seats in the house, they had the majority with 167 seats.

After the election results showed a clear victory for the Awami League, General Yahya Khan and Bhutto were faced with the challenge of how to prevent Mujibur from becoming the Prime Minister. They resorted to various political tactics, and one of which was to persuade Mujibur to form a coalition with Bhutto, who had failed to win any seats in East Pakistan. However, the Awami League was not interested in this proposition, as they believed that they had earned the right to govern with their clear majority in the National Assembly.

Yahya and Bhutto were reluctant to transfer power to someone from East Pakistan, which they perceived as a minority region. They were determined to hold on to power, and this led to a political deadlock. Yahya Khan postponed the scheduled session of the National Assembly, which was supposed to be held in Dhaka on March 3, 1971, to buy more time to find a solution. This move only heightened tensions, and further tested the patience of the Bengalis of East Pakistan.

The situation worsened when Yahya and Bhutto rejected Mujibur's Six-Point Program, which aimed at securing greater autonomy for East Pakistan. The leaders of West Pakistan refused to accept the legitimate demands of the people of East Pakistan, which fueled resentment and frustration among the Bengalis. The stage was set for a showdown between the military regime of West Pakistan and the political leadership of East Pakistan.

The situation in Pakistan was being closely monitored by India, which was wary of any potential conflict or aggression from Pakistan. The Indian intelligence agency, RAW, was particularly vigilant, knowing that the Pakistan military might launch an attack on India to divert attention from the domestic political situation.

In this context, R.N. Kao, the head of RAW, prepared a 25-page secret document addressed to the Cabinet Secretary, outlining India's options in the event of a military conflict with Pakistan. The document considered a range of scenarios, including a limited conflict, a full-scale war, and the possibility of China intervening on Pakistan's behalf. The document also proposed various strategies to counter Pakistan's military capabilities, including the use of air power and Special Forces operations, as well as diplomatic efforts to isolate Pakistan internationally. It highlighted the need for India to be prepared for any eventuality and maintain a strong defensive posture.

In the secret letter addressed to the cabinet secretary, Kao not only warned about the possibility of a military attack from Pakistan, but also mentioned that Pakistan was in the final stages of negotiations with the United States for the purchase of advanced weaponry. He further added that Pakistan was continuously trying to improve its military hardware by purchasing weapons from various countries, which could pose a significant threat to India's security.

During the same period, India was also preparing for the upcoming general election, which was a significant event for the country. Despite being occupied with the election campaign, Prime Minister Indira Gandhi kept herself updated on every development in East Pakistan through her advisors, P.N. Haksar and R.N. Kao. Both Haksar and Kao were regularly providing updates to Indira Gandhi on thc situation in East Pakistan, and they knew that Pakistan was on the brink of collapse, which could potentially lead to an attack on India. Given the delicate situation, India had to be cautious and keep a close eye on the developments across the border. To counter the potential threat of a Pakistani attack, India's ambassador in Moscow was given the responsibility of acquiring the military equipment needed to defend India in a worst-case scenario. This was done in anticipation of the possibility that Pakistan might escalate the situation and launch an attack on India. The Indian government took this threat very seriously, and made sure to take steps to protect the country. By acquiring the necessary military equipment, India was preparing to defend itself and its citizens against any aggression from Pakistan.

Haksar was aware that India needed urgent military assistance and that only the Soviet Union could provide such help. Also in addition to it, realizing the gravity of the situation, Haksar sought permission from Indira Gandhi to form a five-member committee to address the problems arising in East Pakistan. The committee was chaired by the Cabinet Secretary and included Haksar, Kao, the Home Minister, and the Foreign Secretary. Their main objective was to find a solution to the ongoing crisis in East Pakistan, and to provide regular updates to Indira Gandhi.

The five-person committee, which Haksar presided over, met in order to evaluate the potential repercussions for India's standing in the international community that could result from their decision to recognize Bangladesh as an independent nation. The topic of whether or not India should recognize Bangladesh was a delicate subject for the country because it had the potential to strain relations with Pakistan and other countries. The committee was well-aware that the decision they made would not only have an effect on the relationship between India and Pakistan, but would also have far-reaching repercussions for the region as a whole.

The potential effects of recognizing Bangladesh on the economy was another factor taken into consideration by the committee members. They did a cost-benefit analysis to determine the impact that this would have on trade between India and Pakistan as well as the rest of the world. They were aware that this choice would have a significant impact on the nation's foreign policy, and as a result, they wanted to examine all of the potential outcomes and situations before settling on one.

The political ramifications of recognizing Bangladesh was another factor that the committee deliberated upon. They were aware that it would be a risky action that had the ability to either improve India's standing on the international stage or perhaps cut it off from the rest of the international community. Before making a proposal to the Prime Minister, the committee wanted to make sure that they had thoroughly considered all of the relevant factors since they were aware that their choice would have far-reaching consequences.

The committee as a whole came to the conclusion that recognizing Bangladesh's status as an independent nation would have substantial repercussions for India. On the other hand, they were aware that India needed to take a stand on the issue since it could not ignore the humanitarian crisis that was occurring in East Pakistan. They were aware that it was a delicate matter that required handling with care, taking into consideration all of the potential scenarios.. Helping East Pakistan also meant direct conflict with the rest of Pakistan, and that meant inviting war.

When things were being discussed in India on how they could take the matter forward with East Pakistan, RAW had already activated in the region to get insider information.

Indian diplomats were also being sent to East Pakistan to keep the confidence alive within them that were not alone in this fight. One name that came out in this regard was 'Nath Babu'. P.N. Banerjee was an IPS officer of the West Bengal cadre.

Banerjee, also known as Prasanta Nath Banerjee or Nath Babu, was an Indian Police Service (IPS) officer who played a crucial role in the liberation of Bangladesh in 1971.

Before the Bangladesh Liberation, Banerjee had a distinguished career in the Indian Police Service. He was born in 1925 in Calcutta and completed his education at Presidency College, Calcutta. He then joined the Indian Police Service in 1948 and was assigned to the undivided Bengal cadre.

Banerjee quickly established himself as an efficient police officer with a strong sense of duty. He served in various capacities in West Bengal, including as the Deputy Commissioner of Police in Calcutta. He was known for his tough stance against criminals and for his innovative strategies to tackle crime.

P.N. Banerjee played a crucial role in the formation and development of India's external intelligence agency, the Research and Analysis Wing (RAW). In the early 1960s, he was appointed as the deputy director of RAW, where he worked under the legendary intelligence officer, Rameshwar Nath Kao. Banerjee was responsible for building and strengthening the agency's capabilities in areas, such as espionage, counterintelligence, and covert operations.

Banerjee was given a crucial task by RAW chief R.N. Kao during the East Pakistan crisis. Kao assigned him the responsibility of gaining the confidence of Sheikh Mujibur Rahman, the leader of the Awami League in East Pakistan. Banerjee was given a new identity as P. Nath, and was sent to East Pakistan with a new passport to work as a RAW agent.

It was a challenging task for P. Nath to establish contact with Mujibur, who was under constant surveillance by Pakistani intelligence. After numerous attempts, Nath was finally able to arrange a meeting with Mujibur in London in 1968 through his contacts and friends in Pakistan. Over time, Nath gained Mujibur's trust and became his eyes and ears in East Pakistan, providing valuable information to RAW.

P.N. Banerjee's contribution to RAW during the East Pakistan crisis was significant. His efforts helped RAW in gaining crucial information about the Pakistani military's plans and movements in the region. His work as a RAW agent was instrumental in India's eventual victory in the Bangladesh Liberation War.

Unfortunately, on 24th July 1974, Nath Babu passed away suddenly. His untimely demise was a huge loss for RAW, as he was considered one of the agency's most trusted and effective agents. Despite his short life, his contribution to Indian intelligence remains a significant chapter in the history of RAW.

According to a book written by the son of P.N. Banerjee, a former journalist in Kolkata, his father played a crucial role in gaining the trust of Sheikh Mujibur Rahman. As per the book, Banerjee and Mujibur were turning out to be the best of friends, and Mujibur trusted him to an exceptional level. In fact, after the liberation of Bangladesh, Mujibur had invited Banerjee's entire family to his house in Dhaka, and had said that Banerjee was the only non-family member who had full access to his house. This trust was a testament to the invaluable contribution made by Banerjee in keeping Kao informed throughout the Bangladesh Liberation War.

Banerjee's inputs were crucial in keeping Kao on his toes throughout and before the war, and this responsibility was giving Kao sleepless nights. The details that were coming in from across the border were terrifying, and it was Kao's duty to keep Indira Gandhi informed of the sheer danger that they were about to face from Pakistan. Banerjee's close relationship with Mujibur ensured that Kao had a steady flow of information about the situation on the ground. They had to be ready for anything and everything.

During the time leading up to the Bangladesh Liberation War, the political climate in the Indian subcontinent was fraught with uncertainty and tension. On the one hand, Mujibur Rahman the was seeking full assurance from India that they would support his region in the event of an attack by Pakistan. On the other hand, Indian Prime Minister Indira Gandhi was hesitant to provide unequivocal support to the cause, fearing that it would create further strain relations with Pakistan.

While India was not backing out of the situation, the government was taking a cautious approach. Indira Gandhi understood the gravity of the situation and the potential for an all-out war with Pakistan. It was a fragile balance between supporting the cause of East Pakistan's independence and avoiding war with their neighbouring country.

Mujibur Rahman, however, was not satisfied with India's vague assurances and wrote twice to Indira Gandhi, seeking concrete support. This further compounded the already precarious situation, as the tensions between India and Pakistan were at an all-time high. The possibility of a war was looming, and the stakes were high.

As the situation continued to escalate, it was becoming clear that the volcano was about to burst. The fate of East Pakistan hung in the balance, and the Indian government had to navigate the complex political landscape to provide support without provoking a military confrontation with Pakistan.

❑

Formation of Bangladesh

The political situation in West Pakistan and East Pakistan was highly tense and uncertain during the early months of 1971. The Awami League, led by Sheikh Mujibur Rahman, was becoming increasingly restless and demanding autonomy for East Pakistan. However, President Yahya Khan was reluctant to give in to their demands, as it would lead to a loss of power for his own party.

In an attempt to break the deadlock, Mujibur decided to take matters into his own hands. He announced on February 13, 1971, that he would be heading the National Assembly session, with the aim of framing a new constitution for Pakistan that would give greater autonomy to East Pakistan. This move was seen as a direct challenge to Yahya's authority, and sparked a new wave of unrest and protests across the region.

Mujibur's decision to organize the national assembly was quickly rejected by Bhutto. He accused Mujibur of violating democratic principles by trying to impose a one-sided constitution on West Pakistan. Bhutto believed that such a constitution would only benefit the East Pakistanis, leaving West Pakistanis underrepresented and marginalized.

As a result, Bhutto boycotted the decision of Mujibur and organized a mass protest in West Pakistan, calling it a "Black Day". This protest marked the beginning of a long-standing political feud between Bhutto and Mujibur. Now was the time when both parties were clearly coming out on the road to protest against each other.

Bhutto's refusal to accept Mujibur's proposal added to the already existing tension between East and West Pakistan, and escalated the situation towards violence. Bhutto worked towards persuading the people of West Pakistan that what Mujibur was proposing went against their personal interests as Pakistanis. He argued that if the constitution proposed by Mujibur was implemented throughout the country, it would obstruct the growth of democracy. Bhutto's efforts were aimed at retaining the existing power structures in West Pakistan and ensuring that his own interests and those of his supporters were not threatened by the implementation of Mujibur's proposal. This further exacerbated the already fragile relationship between the two regions, and eventually led to the outbreak of war.

"We are not going to Dhaka to return with humiliation," Bhutto quoted.

The situation in East Pakistan was becoming increasingly volatile, as people grew more and more vexed with the lack of progress in their demand for greater autonomy. The decision to call off the national assembly only added fuel to the fire, and then led to widespread unrest on the streets of Dhaka.

As the situation threatened to spiral out of control, Mujibur Rahman found himself in a difficult position. On the one hand, he was seen as the champion of the people's aspirations for greater freedom and autonomy. On the other hand, he was also aware of the risks involved in openly advocating for complete independence from Pakistan.

Despite the mounting pressure from the crowds, Mujibur carefully refrained from making any explicit calls for independence. Instead, he spoke in general terms about the need for greater autonomy and self-determination for the people of East Pakistan.

Mujibur was known for his political acumen and strategic thinking. He was aware that any violent protest could lead to a major loss of lives, and he did not want the situation to escalate to that level. Instead, he wanted to maintain a peaceful environment, and urged his supporters to remain calm and avoid any kind of violent agitation.

In order to achieve this, Mujibur called for 'satyagraha', a non-violent resistance movement that had been successfully employed by Mahatma Gandhi during India's struggle for independence. 'Satyagraha' is a Sanskrit word that means "holding onto truth," and it involves peaceful protest, civil disobedience, and non-cooperation with authorities.

By calling for 'satyagraha', Mujibur was emphasizing the importance of peaceful resistance in achieving their goal of independence. He knew that if the people of East Pakistan could remain united and maintain a peaceful protest, it would be difficult for the Pakistani government to suppress their demands.

However, not all the activists and protesters in East Pakistan were on board with Mujibur's approach. The radicals were not satisfied with the peaceful protests, and wanted more forceful action to achieve their goals. They believed that the only way to end the suffering of the Bengali people was through a full-fledged revolution, even if it meant resorting to violence.

These radical groups were not interested in maintaining any balance or engaging in peaceful dialogue with the Pakistani authorities. They wanted to escalate the conflict, and were determined to fight for complete independence from Pakistan. This led to a sharp division among the Bengali people, with some calling for non-violent protests and others advocating for more militant actions.

As tensions continued to rise, the situation in East Pakistan became increasingly precarious, and the radical elements started to gain more power and influence among the population. The movement for independence was becoming more and more radicalized, and the seeds of a violent conflict were being sown.

The growing tension between Yahya and Mujibur had reached a boiling point, and it was evident to the public that the two leaders were on opposite sides of the political spectrum. Yahya's speeches were becoming excessively critical of Mujibur, and he held him responsible for the fuelling unrest in Pakistan. Adding to this, Yahya sent a secret letter to Mujibur, urging him to reconsider his position.

While Yahya tried to persuade Mujibur to change his stance, he was also considering regarding the imposition of martial law again. This decision would mean that all powers would be concentrated in Yahya's hands, and the country would be ruled through military governance. The idea of martial law was controversial, and many Pakistanis did not favour it. However, Yahya was running out of options and believed this might be the only way to quell the unrest in East Pakistan.

The situation was becoming increasingly tense, and the fate of East Pakistan hung in the balance. The decisions by Yahya and Mujibur in the coming days would determine the course of history for Pakistan.

On March 7, 1971, Mujibur Rahman gave what became known as the "Bangabandhu Speech" at the Racecourse Ground in Dhaka. In the speech, he said that East Pakistan should be free, and called for a movement of non-cooperation to fight against the Pakistani government. The West Pakistani ruling class had been mistreating the Bengali people for too long. This speech was a powerful call-to-arms and action for the Bengali people, and resonated with them deeply. The people in the crowd were ecstatic, and they waved the flags of an independent Bangladesh with great enthusiasm.

In his speech, Mujibur Rahman laid out his vision for a new Bangladesh that was based on democracy, equality, and justice. He spoke about the injustices faced by the Bengali people, their economic exploitation, and their cultural suppression. He also criticized the policies of the West Pakistani government, and accused them of discriminating against the Bengali people.

Bengali people saw Mujibur as their leader and rallied behind him in large numbers. The speech also inspired artists, poets, and musicians to create works celebrating Bengali culture and identity.

Mujibur's speech was a turning point in the fight for Bangladeshi freedom, and it was clear that he had taken control of the eastern part of Pakistan. But Yahya Khan refused to accept the situation, and kept saying that Mujibur was to blame for the trouble in the country. He even sent Mujibur a secret letter telling him to change his mind. Yahya was also thinking about putting martial law in place to stop the growing nationalism in East Pakistan.

In answer to what Mujibur said, Yahya moved the date of his trip to Dhaka from March 10 to March 15. Mujibur didn't like this move because he thought it showed disrespect. Tensions between the two leaders kept rising, and it became clear that a peaceful end to the crisis was becoming less possible.

On March 16, 1971, General Yahya Khan arrived in Dhaka, supposedly for negotiations with Mujibur Rahman to resolve the political crisis. However, it soon became apparent that Yahya did not intend to grant autonomy to East Pakistan or accommodate Mujibur's demands. In fact, the real purpose of Yahya's visit was to assess the level of preparedness of the East Pakistani military, and gather intelligence on the situation on the ground.

Yahya brought with him a team of generals to assess the military capability of East Pakistan and to decide on a course of action. The Pakistani army had been planning a military crackdown against the Bengali people, and Yahya's visit was seen as the final go-ahead for this brutal operation.

General Tikka Khan, known as the "Butcher of Bengal," was appointed by President Yahya Khan to lead the military crackdown in East Pakistan. He assured Yahya Khan that he could restore normalcy to the region within a week, but his plan was ruthless and brutal.

The first step in the plan was to expel all foreign media and TV crews from the region. Journalists from international news organizations were targeted, with many of them being manhandled and forced to leave the country. The aim was to prevent any coverage of the atrocities being committed in East Pakistan from reaching the outside world. As a result, the outside world was kept largely unaware of the bloody military crackdown that was about to unfold.

Despite the efforts of the Pakistani military, news of the atrocities eventually leaked out to the world, owing in part to the work of courageous journalists who risked their lives to report on the situation. Many of these journalists took refuge in neighbouring India, which would eventually play a key role in the liberation of Bangladesh.

The night of 25 March 1971 is known as one of the darkest moments in the history of Bangladesh. General Tikka Khan led the brutal crackdown on East Pakistan. The operation was planned with the aim to crush the independence movement in the region and to ensure the unity of Pakistan.

The crackdown began at 11 p.m., and Tikka Khan was in-charge of the operation. The Pakistani army launched a massive assault on unarmed civilians, students of universities, and supporters of the Awami League who were out on the streets.

They were mercilessly gunned down, and many were also beaten to death. The military used tanks, machine guns, and other heavy weaponry to quell the uprising.

The streets of Dhaka were littered with the dead bodies of innocent people. It is estimated that between 7,000 to 10,000 people were killed during the operation. Many women were also raped, and countless people were injured. The operation was carried out with complete impunity, and no one could stop the military from committing these heinous crimes.

It was one of the very few military operations that took place to scare people away from their demands.

The Pakistani Army's operation to crush the Bengali nationalist movement began with the assault on Iqbal Hall in Dhaka University, a political activity hotbed. Tanks and troops were sent to the location to clear the space, and the Army began a ruthless crackdown on the unarmed students and civilians there.

However, the Army's tactics soon escalated to even more barbaric levels. In an effort to create a sense of fear and intimidation among the local population, they set fire to the surrounding slums. These slums were home to thousands of poor men and their families who had sought refuge against railway lines. The fires quickly spread, and the resulting conflagration claimed the lives of thousands of innocent people who had no connection to the political unrest. It was a callous and inhumane tactic, showing the depths to which the Pakistani Army was willing to stoop to achieve its goals.

This assault on Iqbal Hall and the subsequent attack on the slums began a sustained campaign of violence and terror in East Pakistan. The Army went from village to village, rounding up suspected Bengali nationalists and executing them on the spot.

The violence and brutality of the military operation were widespread, and the Bengali population suffered greatly. Many teachers and their families were killed within the university, including Hindus who were prime targets. The army was indiscriminately killing, with reports of soldiers breaking into homes and shooting unarmed civilians. The situation was chaotic, with people running for their lives and seeking refuge wherever they could.

When news of this slaughter reached Mujibur Rahman, he knew he had to act. He told all his leaders to go underground, and did not wait to counter-attack. He wanted to go on radio and declare independence, but the military had already taken down the Dhaka radio station.

After realizing that the Dhaka radio station was already taken down, Mujibur Rahman made a bold move and headed to the Chittagong Radio station, which was still operational at the time. He saw this as a crucial opportunity to declare East Pakistan's independence, and send a message to the rest of the world.

Upon arriving at the radio station, Mujibur declared East Pakistan's independence over EPR wireless. He urged the people of Bangladesh to resist the military attack, and fight back if necessary until the last Pakistani soldier leaves their land. Mujibur's words were powerful and inspiring, and his message resonated with the Bengali people, who were determined to defend their land and their freedom.

Chittagong Radio, being the only operational radio station at the time, was quick to respond to Mujibur's declaration of independence. Within the next few hours, the news of East Pakistan's independence spread like wildfire, and everyone knew about the situation in East Pakistan.

Mujibur's declaration of independence marked a turning point in the Bangladesh Liberation War, and his words served as a beacon of hope for the Bengali people, who were facing barbarous military attacks. His courage and determination to fight for the rights and freedoms of his people inspired countless others to join the cause and resist the oppression of the Pakistani army.

After Mujibur's declaration of independence, the Pakistani army started a well-planned and inhuman operation to suppress any resistance. Mujibur was quickly arrested, and other leaders went into hiding. The military crackdown was so thorough that for the first few days, the world remained unaware of what was happening in Bangladesh.

However, a few journalists managed to escape the Pakistani military's clutches, including Simon Dring of the Daily Telegraph. He was staying in a hotel in Dhaka when the crackdown began. He evaded the attack by hiding on the roof of his hotel, where he could witness the horrors unfolding on the streets below.

When Dring got the opportunity to escape, he filled out a chilling report describing the massacre's extent. He claimed that within the first 24 hours of the military crackdown, at least 7,000 people were killed in Dhaka alone, and the number of casualties in all of Bangladesh was nearly 15,000. These reports shocked the world, and it became clear that the Pakistani military was carrying out a ruthless genocide against the Bengali people.

On March 27, after 33 hours of curfew, the residents of Dhaka were finally able to leave the city. However, the situation outside of Dhaka was just as grim. The Pakistani army continued their killing spree in Chittagong, Jessore, and Comilla. They also used their air force to bomb more than 15,000 villages across East Pakistan. It is difficult to estimate the exact number of casualties, but it is believed that around one million people lost their lives in this genocide.

The mass exodus from Dhaka led to the displacement of almost 10 million people who fled to neighbouring India as refugees. This created a humanitarian crisis, as India struggled to accommodate and provide aid to such a large number of people.

The Pakistani army also targeted intellectuals, academics and cultural figures, who they saw as a threat to their rule. They systematically killed anyone who had the potential to be a leader or a voice of dissent. This included doctors, journalists, poets, writers, and musicians.

The atrocities committed by the Pakistani army in East Pakistan were so savage and widespread that they have been compared to the Holocaust. This was an extermination of unprecedented scale and magnitude. The international community was slow to respond to the crisis, with many countries reluctant to interfere in the internal affairs of Pakistan.

India's response to the crisis in East Pakistan was significant, as it was the only country that took immediate action to address the situation. The Indian parliament convened to discuss the issue, and on 31 March, they passed a unanimous resolution demanding that the Pakistani military withdraw immediately from East Pakistan. This demonstrated India's strong stance against the atrocities committed in Bangladesh and their unwavering support for their fellow South Asian countrymen.

The refugee crisis was also a major issue that India had to contend with. As the violence in East Pakistan escalated, the number of refugees crossing the border into India grew exponentially. By the end of July, there were around 10 million refugees in India, putting a significant strain on resources and infrastructure of the country. The government had to quickly mobilize resources to provide food, shelter and medical assistance to many of the refugees who needed help.

The refugee crisis was not only a humanitarian issue, but also a political one. India's relationship with Pakistan was strained, and the influx of refugees added further tension between the two countries. The Indian government had to balance its responsibility to protect the refugees with the need to maintain diplomatic relations with Pakistan and other neighbouring countries.

Despite the challenges, India remained committed to supporting the refugees and providing aid to Bangladesh. Indian volunteers and aid providers worked tirelessly to assist those in need, and the Indian government continued to put pressure on the international community to take action and condemn the atrocities being committed in East Pakistan.

On the 31March, two influential leaders of the Awami League, Tajuddin Ahmad and Amirul Islam, crossed the Indian border secretly. They were caught by the Border Security Force (BSF) and were first taken to Calcutta, and then to Delhi to meet with the Indian Prime Minister to discuss the situation in East Pakistan in detail.

The Awami League leaders and other Bengalis from around the world were willing to contribute to the war effort. Tajuddin Ahmad and other leaders knew that to survive in this war, they needed to have a well-organized resistance movement, and they were not seeking mere sympathy. They wanted India's help to secure their land and fight back against the Pakistani military.

Tajuddin Ahmad and other Awami League leaders also realized the importance of organizing the Bengali population in East Pakistan to resist the Pakistani military. On 10 April 1971, all the leaders and representatives of East Pakistan came on a single stage. They discussed the needs in detail. Finally, under the leadership of Tajuddin, they formed a provisional government called the Mujibnagar Government, which was located in the town of Mujibnagar in East Pakistan (now Bangladesh). This government was formed to provide political leadership and direction to the Bengali resistance movement, and became the symbol of Bengali resistance against the Pakistani military.

Tajuddin Ahmad played a crucial role in leading the fight for Bangladesh's independence from Pakistan. In the absence of Mujibur Rahman, who was arrested by the Pakistani army, Tajuddin became the de facto leader of the Awami League and the independence movement.

Recognizing Tajuddin's leadership potential, the Indian government worked with him and other leaders to form a provisional government for Bangladesh. This government was formally established on April 17, 1971, in the village of Baidyanathtala, which was later renamed Mujibnagar in honour of Sheikh Mujibur Rahman. Tajuddin became the Prime Minister of the provisional government, and he worked tirelessly to organize the Bengali resistance against the Pakistani army, and secure international recognition for Bangladesh's independence. That day, Tajuddin appealed to the world to recognize Bangladesh as an independent country. He said on the stage that now 'Pakistan is dead and buried under the mountain of corpses. The millions who got killed will always stand like a barrier between West Pakistan and Bangladesh.'

The inspiring words of Tajuddin Ahmad had a powerful impact on Bengalis all over the world. Many who had previously served Pakistan began to change their loyalties and support Bangladesh's cause for independence. This sentiment was particularly strong among Bengalis who were posted in foreign countries as ambassadors and other officials. In total, around 126 Bengalis who were serving in diplomatic posts across the world left their positions and pledged their support to Bangladesh.

These individuals were stationed in countries such as the Philippines, India, Iraq and Argentina, and their defection was a significant boost to the morale of the Bengali people. It demonstrated that the cause for independence was not limited to those inside Bangladesh, but was also supported by Bengali people all over the world, who were willing to make personal sacrifices in order to support their fellow countrymen. This act of solidarity helped to galvanize the movement, and gave hope to those fighting for Bangladesh's freedom.

During the Bangladesh Liberation War, the Indian intelligence agency, Research and Analysis Wing (RAW), played a crucial role in providing support to the Bangladeshi freedom fighters. RAW was working tirelessly to process a vast amount of information coming from various sources, including the intelligence reports provided by Nath Babu.

Meanwhile, the Indian Army was also preparing the training ground for the Bangladesh refugees who had fled their country and were seeking refuge in India. The refugees were being trained to fight against the Pakistani military, and the blueprint for the counter-attack was almost ready. Sam Manekshaw, who was the Indian Army Chief at the time, was personally overseeing the training program.

RAW was also involved in coordinating with foreign governments and organizations to provide support to Bangladesh. The agency established contacts with countries, like the United States, Japan and the United Kingdom, to secure weapons and ammunition for the freedom fighters. They also worked with organizations, like OXFAM and Caritas, to provide humanitarian aid to the refugees.

Due to the inputs from Banerjee and other reliable sources, India knew precisely to whom to provide aid to keep the underground forces well-equipped and well-informed in order to fight the Pakistani forces.

The situation in East Pakistan was getting worse day-by-day, and India had to prepare for a potential war with Pakistan. Prime Minister Indira Gandhi was aware of the gravity of the situation, and knew that India had to be fully prepared for any eventuality. To this end, she formed a committee to plan and strategize for the conflict. The committee consisted of several key players, including Rameshwar Nath Kao, the founder of India's external intelligence agency, RAW.

As the situation escalated, the committee was expanded to include K.B. Lall, the Defense Secretary. Kao's role in the committee was crucial, as he was responsible for gathering and processing intelligence from various sources. The army was also preparing for the war, and Sam Manekshaw, the Army Chief, was overseeing the training program for the Bangladeshi refugees.

Indira Gandhi knew that a war with Pakistan would have significant implications for the region and the world. However, they were determined to do whatever it took to help the people of East Pakistan achieve their independence.

Indira Gandhi's dilemma on how to deal with the situation in East Pakistan was not just due to international pressure, but also because of the fear of a possible backlash from China. Kao, being the trusted head of RAW, was able to provide valuable insights and advice to the Prime Minister.

Apart from his intelligence-gathering efforts, Kao's ability to multitask and delegate work to the right people made him an invaluable asset to the government. He was able to stay in touch with various ministries simultaneously, ensuring that everyone was on the same page and working towards a common goal.

One of Kao's important contributions during this time was the establishment of training camps for Mukti Bahini, the Bengali guerrilla fighters who were fighting against the Pakistani army. Kao, along with his team, identified suitable locations, helped coordinate the training programs and provided them with weapons and supplies to prepare them for the impending conflict. The Mukti Bahini played a crucial role in the eventual victory of Bangladesh, and Kao's efforts were instrumental in their training and preparation.

Kao's work during this period also involved keeping a close eye on the movements of the Chinese military, who were reportedly providing support to the Pakistani army. His intelligence reports helped the government understand the scale and nature of China's involvement, and take appropriate measures to counter it.

R.N. Kao's work during the Bangladesh Liberation War was highly commendable. As the head of RAW, Kao played a crucial role in gathering and analyzing intelligence information and developing strategies to support the Bengali struggle for independence. He was known for his ability to keep things organized, even in the midst of chaos.

Kao's work was not limited to the military aspect of the war, but also extended to the diplomatic front. He was instrumental in forging alliances with other countries, including the Soviet Union and the United States, to garner support for India's stance on the Bangladesh issue.

Kao's influence on the war was not limited to his own work, but also extended to the soldiers and civilians on the ground. His leadership and guidance gave them hope and confidence, and his presence was a source of reassurance during the difficult times of the war.

R.N. Kao was renowned for his ability to work behind the scenes and guide others on the course of action. His expertise and guidance proved to be invaluable in many critical situations, and he played an important role in the success of various individuals and groups. One of Kao's strengths was his calm demeanour, which made him a trusted advisor and mentor for many.

Kao's impact was felt beyond the borders of Bangladesh as well. He provided guidance to those who wanted to support the cause of Bangladesh, but were unsure how to do so without putting themselves at risk. He urged them to become vocal supporters, which helped to rally international support for the fight for independence. Kao also provided information to Western media outlets, giving them a first-hand account of the atrocities committed by the Pakistani army in Bangladesh. This helped raise global awareness about the situation in the country, and put pressure on the international community to act.

Sankaran Nair and Kao were not only focused on their individual roles in Bangladesh, but also on their primary responsibility, which was to protect Indian borders. Nair had managed to get a mole within the Pakistani army, which became crucial as the mole provided information that the Pakistanis were planning to attack an Indian forward base on 1 December. Nair shared this information with Kao, who then alerted the Prime Minister. The Indian Air Force was put on high alert, but nothing happened on the anticipated date. Even on 2 December, there was no sign of an attack. However, on Nair's request, the Air Headquarters decided to maintain the alert for one more day, and on 3 December, Pakistan attacked. Thanks to the preparedness of the Indian Air Force, the Pakistani mission failed miserably. The Indian Air Force's vigilance and readiness to tackle any situation proved to be a game-changer in thwarting the enemy's plans. The anticipated attack date may have been delayed, but the Indian Air Force was well-prepared to counter any aggression.

Later, when Nair thought about the delay in the date, he realized that it was the mistake of RAW itself. The date provided by the mole was 3December only, but the one who decoded the message read the message wrong, and assumed it to be 1 December.

The same scenario was repeated during the 13-day war with Pakistan, where India had prior information about the attack. As a result, India was able to resist and fight back effectively. Yahya soon released Mujibur after this war, which ultimately resulted in the creation of a new nation. Eventually, he took over Bangladesh, which became an independent nation.

Nair and Kao's vigilance and preparation for defending the Indian borders were crucial in these situations. Their efforts helped the Indian Armed Forces prepare and respond effectively to the enemy's attacks. The creation of Bangladesh marked a significant moment in the history of South Asia, as it was the first time that a new nation was formed on the basis of linguistic and cultural differences. Nair and Kao's contribution to this process highlights the importance of strategic planning and preparedness in maintaining national security.

❑

The Sikkim Story

The successful liberation of Bangladesh not only became a success story for India, but also a turning point in the history of South Asia. India's role as a major regional power was established, and it gained significant influence and recognition on the global stage. The success of the liberation of Bangladesh boosted Indira Gandhi's political stature, and made her a popular leader, not only in India but also across the world. It also helped to improve India's relations with other countries, including the United States and China.

The United States, which had been hesitant to support India's intervention in East Pakistan, began to take India more seriously as a regional power. In fact, the US later played a crucial role in mediating between India and Pakistan, leading to the signing of the Simla Agreement in 1972. This agreement helped to resolve several outstanding issues between the two countries, including the issue of prisoners of war, and the return of occupied territories.

China, on the other hand, did not intervene in the war and remained neutral. This was partly due to its own concerns about the situation in its own eastern wing, Tibet. However, China was also happy that India had taken the lead in resolving the conflict, as it did not want to be seen as interfering in the internal affairs of other countries. The success of India's intervention in Bangladesh also helped to improve India-China relations, which had been tense since the 1962 border conflict.

Despite the significant victory in the Bangladesh war, Indira Gandhi was aware of the pressing issues that required immediate attention within the country's borders. She understood that there was no time to revel in the triumph and that there were many other challenges that needed to be addressed. One of the major problems that needed her attention was the growing crisis in Sikkim. The state, located between Bhutan and Tibet, had a strategic position on India's border, making it crucial for the country's security.

The Treaty of 1950 between India and Sikkim made Sikkim an Indian protectorate, and gave India control over its external affairs, defense, and communications. However, the Chogyal, the king of Sikkim, wanted to renegotiate the treaty to regain some of the powers he had lost. This created a tricky situation for India, as any move to give in to the Chogyal's demands could lead to China's interference in the region.

The Chogyal had requested that India revise the treaty signed in 1950. This request was a major cause of concern for Indira Gandhi's government, as any changes in the treaty could potentially weaken India's control over Sikkim and threaten its security.

Thus, Indira Gandhi had to navigate this delicate situation with great caution and strategic planning. She understood the importance of maintaining India's hold on Sikkim, while also addressing the concerns and demands of the Chogyal. The situation required skillful negotiation and diplomacy, and Indira Gandhi was the person for this task.

Before we begin, let us revisit the events of 1947 that became the origin of this problem.

Sardar Vallabhbhai Patel played a crucial role in the integration of the princely states into an independent India. In 1947, when India gained independence, there were over 500 princely states that were not part of British India. Sardar Patel was appointed as the Deputy Prime Minister and the Home Minister of India, and his primary responsibility was to bring these princely states into the Indian Union.

Sardar Patel used a combination of diplomacy and strength to achieve the integration of the princely states. He first tried to negotiate with the rulers of these states and convince them to join India. He promised them that they would retain their privileges and autonomy, but they would have to accept the sovereignty of India. Sardar Patel believed that it was essential to integrate these princely states into India to strengthen the unity and integrity of the country.

However, not all princely states were willing to join India. Some of them, like Hyderabad and Kashmir, were particularly resistant to the idea. In these cases, Sardar Patel used force to integrate them into India. For example, he ordered the Indian army to invade Hyderabad in 1948, which led to the integration of the state into India. Similarly, in the case of Kashmir, Sardar Patel convinced the Maharaja to accede to India, and the Indian army was sent to the state to fight off the Pakistani invaders.

In the case of Sikkim, which was a protectorate of India, the situation was different. The 1950 treaty also stated that Sikkim would consult India before entering any external relations. However, in the 1960s, the Chogyal demanded more autonomy, whichled to a political crisis in Sikkim, and India had to intervene to restore order.

Jawaharlal Nehru's approach towards Sikkim was to give it special treatment, but this decision was not supported by everyone, including Indira Gandhi. In hindsight, it can be seen as a mistake to have treated Sikkim differently from other states in India.

Sikkim was a strategically important state, sandwiched between Bhutan and Tibet, and its border with China was a sensitive issue. Despite this, Nehru believed in giving the Sikkimese monarch a significant degree of autonomy, and he even allowed the Chogyal to retain his title and powers after India gained independence in 1947. This was in contrast to Patel's approach of integrating all princely states into India without any special treatment. However, this approach of treating Sikkim differently proved to be problematic in the long run.

Sikkim, despite being a small state, has had a long history of political intrigue and maneuvering. In the early 1950s and 1960s, Sikkim was going through a period of heightened political activity, with various individuals and groups vying for power. One of the key figures during this time was Kazi Lhendup Dorjee, popularly known as "Kazi Sahib." He was a prominent political leader who played an important role in Sikkim's struggle for democracy and self-rule.

Kazi Sahib was a strong advocate of democracy and believed that the people of Sikkim should have the right to elect their own leaders. He worked tirelessly to promote the idea of democracy in Sikkim and was instrumental in the formation of the Sikkim State Congress, a political party that aimed to bring democratic reforms to the state.

However, not everyone in Sikkim shared Kazi Sahib's vision for the future. There were powerful interests within the state that were opposed to democracy and wanted to maintain the status quo. This led to a lot of political tension and uncertainty, with frequent changes in leadership and shifting alliances.

The situation in Sikkim was becoming increasingly tense as the Chogyal demanded full sovereignty for the state. India, on the other hand, was not willing to grant complete independence to the small Himalayan state due to its strategic location between Bhutan and Tibet. Indira Gandhi, the Prime Minister of India, sought the help of her trusted advisors, R.N. Kao and P.N. Haksar, to find a solution to the issue.

In December 1972, Kao asked for a fortnight to revert to Gandhi with a plan of action. During this time, Kao and Haksar strategized and devised a plan to remove the Chogyal from power, and merge Sikkim with India. Kao met with the Chief Secretary of Sikkim and advised him to hold off on any decisions until further notice.

After the successful Bangladesh mission, Kao sought the help of his trusted associate, Banerjee, to deal with the Sikkim issue. Together, they worked on a plan to persuade the Chogyal to agree to India's demands or accept complete merger with India. Banerjee, who was enthusiastic about this new mission, returned to Delhi within 10 days with Ajit Singh Syali, a member of RAW who was posted on special duty in Gangtok. Syali's expertise and knowledge of the local situation made him an invaluable asset to the team. They worked together to devise a strategy to resolve the Sikkim issue and bring it under the control of the Indian government.

Banerjee, who held dual positions in both the Intelligence Bureau (IB) and the Research and Analysis Wing (RAW), presented his plan to Kao upon returning to India. He informed Kao that the merger of Sikkim with India was possible but would require some time. Kao immediately briefed Prime Minister Indira Gandhi and her trusted aide Haksar about the plan. Although Gandhi gave the green light to proceed, she also wanted Foreign Secretary Kewal Singh to be involved in the mission. However, she specifically instructed Kao to keep Singh in the dark about the merger aspect of the plan.

Banerjee's plan was to erode the Chogyal's authority in Sikkim by leveraging the leadership of influential figures such as Kazi. The plan required extensive groundwork, such as building a network of agents and informants who could gather intelligence and disseminate propaganda in Sikkim. Kao, Banerjee, and Syali, started working together to implement the plan. They began by gathering information and building relationships with key players in Sikkim's political landscape.

Banerjee, being a man with many contacts, used his network to agitate the leaders of Sikkim, and encourage them to take to the streets to demand more power, thus creating an air of unrest against their own ruler, the Chogyal. Syali, who was well-versed in the situation in Sikkim, took charge of mobilizing the people's desire for India. The operation was set in motion in early 1973, at a time when there was already unrest within Sikkim due to various local issues, such as job opportunities, income inequalities, discrimination, and other grievances.

RAW found the timing of the mission to be opportune, as it allowed them to capitalize on the existing discontent among the people of Sikkim, and use it to further their goal of integrating the region with India. Banerjee's plan was to weaken the Chogyal's empire by creating a popular movement that would demand greater autonomy for Sikkim. The ultimate goal was to convince the Chogyal to accede to India or face the possibility of a complete merger with India, thereby extinguishing his sovereignty over Sikkim.

While Kewal Singh was kept out of the loop on the merger plan, he was tasked with creating an atmosphere of diplomatic pressure on the Chogyal, which would eventually lead him to agree to India's terms.

Kazi Lhendup Dorjee was a prominent figure in Sikkimese politics and a natural leader. He was widely popular among the people of Sikkim due to his efforts in addressing their grievances and improving their lives. In February 1973, Kazi joined hands with K.C. Pradhan of the Janata Congress to form a united front against the Chogyal. It was not a sudden union, but Banerjee was the mastermind behind this as well. He was the one who made these two leaders become one. The new front was named the Joint Action Committee (JAC). This was a significant development in Sikkimese politics, as it brought together two major opposition groups to challenge the Chogyal's authority.

The JAC launched a campaign demanding political reforms and greater representation for the people of Sikkim. They called for the establishment of a democratic government and the end of the Chogyal's autocratic rule. Kazi played a key role in mobilizing the masses and organizing protests and demonstrations. The JAC's demands gained widespread support among the people, and their campaign put immense pressure on the Chogyal to address their concerns.

As the JAC's campaign gained momentum, Kao and Banerjee continued to work behind the scenes to further their mission to merge Sikkim with India. They saw the JAC's demands as an opportunity to weaken the Chogyal's authority and push for Sikkim's integration with India. Syali, who was on the ground in Sikkim, also played a critical role in gaining support for the JAC's demands and pushing for Sikkim's merger with India.

In March 1973, Banerjee updated Kao on the situation in Sikkim, and informed him that the activities of the Joint Action Committee (JAC) had turned the region into a hotbed of tension. Banerjee reported that there were large-scale protests taking place in front of the palace, which were creating a lot of tension in the region. Banerjee also told Kao that because of these protests, the Chogyal has been quite unnerved.

Banerjee was informed about the role of the Central Intelligence Agency (CIA) in the unfolding situation in Sikkim. According to Banerjee, there was a US consultant named Peter Burley based in Calcutta who had been granted a special audience with the Chogyal. During their meeting, the Chogyal reportedly hinted that he may be willing to seek India's assistance to quell the growing protests and agitations in Sikkim.

Banerjee also learned that the Chogyal was attempting to negotiate with Kazi, the popular leader of the Sikkim National Congress (SNC), by organizing a one-on-one meeting with him. Despite this, Banerjee himself was confident that Kazi would never abandon his agenda and ally with the Chogyal, as Kazi enjoyed tremendous popularity among the people of Sikkim, and was seen as a champion of their cause.

Banerjee's revelation about the CIA's involvement added a new dimension to the situation, as India had long been wary of foreign interference in its internal affairs. It also highlighted the complex web of political intrigue and diplomatic maneuvering that was at play in the region. Nevertheless, Banerjee remained undeterred and focused on his mission to weaken the Chogyal's grip on power, and pave the way for Sikkim's eventual integration into India.

In a high-level meeting attended by Foreign Secretary Kewal Singh, Defense Secretary K.B. Lall, Home Minister Govind Narain, R.N. Kao, Director North in the MEA, and Banerjee, it was decided to remove the protective layer that supported the Chogyal. There were talks of getting some of the districts merged with India, but the idea was rejected outright. The team then discussed how to proceed over the situation, and several ideas were put forward.

One of the primary strategies was to keep the agitation going until the Chogyal himself comes to India's aid. It was also decided to let the people of Sikkim know that the King of Sikkim is not the legal heir of the throne. According to the discussions in the meeting, the elder brother's elder son of the last king should have been the true king. This fact was to be highlighted in the local newspapers to inform the people of Sikkim that the best way to get out of their insufferable condition was to get India's support.

Another important decision made during the meeting was to send Indian army troops on regular marches when the unrest became unbearable, so that people could see that India was always there to help. These marches would help establish India's presence in the region and provide the necessary support to the local people.

It is important to note that these discussions took place at a time when there was a lot of political turmoil in Sikkim. The agitation was growing stronger with each passing day, and the people were looking towards India for support. The meeting aimed at addressing these issues, and come up with a concrete plan to deal with the situation at hand.

RAW's active role in Sikkim was becoming increasingly evident with each passing day. The agency was working relentlessly to maintain a sense of unity between the two parties, SNC and Janata Congress, which were crucial in keeping the Chogyal on his toes. RAW understood that any personal squabble or disagreement between these two parties could jeopardize the entire plan, and thus, took extra care to prevent it from happening.

RAW also realized that keeping the agitations alive was crucial in ensuring that the Chogyal would eventually come to India for help. They had a series of plans in place to keep the momentum going, including publishing articles in local newspapers stating that the King of Sikkim was not the legal heir of the throne.

In the midst of all this, Kazi remained a crucial factor in RAW's plan. RAW understood that Kazi's leadership and support were critical in keeping the agitations alive. They continued to work closely with Kazi, using his network of contacts to further their plan.

Overall, RAW's active involvement in Sikkim was slowly, but surely yielding results. The plan was being executed meticulously, and every action was taken with the end goal in mind—the eventual merger of Sikkim with India.

The events of the 50th birthday of the Chogyal were a turning point in the agitation. The planned demonstrations across Sikkim had resulted in clashes on the streets of Gangtok, and led to police firing that resulted in several deaths. Amidst the chaos, the elder son of the Chogyal tried to come out of the palace, but was stopped by the police. In retaliation, the guards of the prince opened fire on the protestors, which resulted in more casualties.

This incident proved to be a golden opportunity for Kazi to further his agenda. He widened his agitation to include the entire Chogyal family, accusing them of being responsible for the violence. Meanwhile, RAW continued to fan the flames of unrest in Sikkim. They made sure that the protests continued and that the people of Sikkim knew that India was ready to support them in their struggle. Throughout the day, the demonstrations kept on getting violent and that created more problems within the boundaries of Sikkim.

On 6 April, Indira Gandhi, the then Prime Minister of India, held a meeting with Kewal Singh, the Foreign Secretary, and P.N. Dhar, a close aide and advisor. The topic of discussion was the ongoing political crisis in Sikkim. The situation was highly complex, with various parties and stakeholders vying for power and influence.

During the meeting, Indira Gandhi surprised both Singh and Dhar by revealing her stance on the matter within half an hour of the discussion. It was clear that she had already made up her mind on how to proceed. She stated that she would accept the request of the Chogyal as soon as it was made.

The swift decision-making by Indira Gandhi was characteristic of her leadership style. She was known for her decisive actions, and the ability to cut through complex issues with ease. However, her decision was not without controversy. Many believed that her support for the Chogyal went against the wishes of the majority of Sikkimese people who were agitating for democratic reforms and the end of the monarchy.

Finally on 8 April, the Chogyal's request came. After the Chogyal's request to take control of Sikkim administration, the Indian government acted swiftly and efficiently to complete the necessary paperwork and formalities within a day. On the 9 April, the Indian Parliament was informed about the developments in Sikkim.

Kazi was also informed to ease down his agitation as India had taken control of the situation. However, this was just the first phase of the process.

After the successful completion of the first phase, the Indian government moved on to the second phase of the mission. The Ministry of External Affairs (MEA) selected B.S. Das as the Chief Executive of Sikkim to lead the negotiations with the anti-Chogyal forces in the region. Das was given a clear mandate to ensure that the merger with India would be carried out smoothly and that the anti-Chogyal forces would be brought on board.

Das was tasked with the important responsibility of winning over the hearts and minds of the people of Sikkim, and convincing them that their interests would be best served by merging with India. He was also instructed to assure the people that their cultural identity and traditions would be respected and preserved.

One of Das's main objectives was to establish a dialogue with the anti-Chogyal forces in the region and to bring them on board with the merger process. Additionally, Das was instructed to ensure the anti-Chogyal forces that once the merger was complete, the popular party of Sikkim would be given a fair chance to form a government. This was an important step in ensuring that the people of Sikkim felt represented, and that their voices were heard in the new political landscape.

Indira Gandhi was determined to see the complete merger of Sikkim happen as quickly as possible. She was growing increasingly impatient as negotiations dragged on, and she was not alone. The anti-Chogyal parties were also getting restless, eager to see the end of the Chogyal rule, and to take control of Sikkim's political future.

However, R.N. Kao, the director of RAW, had a different perspective. He was concerned that if any third force came into being, the Janata Congress would feel betrayed. To prevent this, he began to work on convincing the people of Sikkim that the Chogyal dynasty was hindering the development of their state. He pointed out that neighboring districts, like Darjeeling were flourishing under India, while Sikkim was not a beneficiary at all.

Kao's approach was aimed at winning over the people of Sikkim to the idea of a merger with India. He wanted them to see that the future of their state was inextricably tied to India, and that their best chance for development and progress lay in becoming a part of the Indian union. This was a delicate balancing act, as Kao did not want to alienate the anti-Chogyal forces, or make them feel like they were being pushed aside.

Over the next six months, as the elections drew near, it was important for the JAC to keep the agitation going. However, amidst all this, Kao received disturbing news. It was reported to him that Chogyal's sister Coocoola and her children were attempting to seek the assistance of the US and UN to press charges against the Indian government. These allegations, if spread, could have potentially derailed the entire mission.

To prevent this from happening, R.N. Kao and his team came up with a plan. They reminded Coocoola that if she continued with her plans, the old case against her involving the illegal export of idols would be reopened. This would not only damage her reputation, but also create problems for the Chogyal family. The warning was enough to deter Coocoola and put an end to her efforts to seek outside help.

The first-ever election in Sikkim was held in April 1975, and it saw a resounding victory for Kazi, who secured 31 out of the 32 seats in the assembly. This result was even beyond the expectations of R.N. Kao, who had been instrumental in orchestrating the merger of Sikkim with India. With Indian supervision, Kazi signed the Government of Sikkim Act 1974, which granted the state the status of an associate state, but this was only the first step towards the actual merger.

Despite the overwhelming victory of Kazi and his party, the actual merger of Sikkim with India was still being awaited. Before the actual merger, many more things were yet to unfold, and the first was the Chogyal's visit to Kathmandu, where he requested the United Nations to intervene in the matter. This move by the Chogyal gave India a reason to take the final steps in the merger plan. It was already planned by India in December 1972 and all the groundwork was already done. Just a nod was required from Indira Gandhi and that too came soon.

The final phase of the merger of Sikkim required careful planning and execution to ensure success. The first step was to disarm the Sikkim Guards, which was scheduled to take place on 8 or 9 April 1975. Prior to this, there needed to be large public meetings in Gangtok demanding the removal of the guards and the merger with India.

During these meetings, the Sikkim Guards were expected to respond by firing or throwing grenades, giving the cabinet the opportunity to take immediate action to remove them from the palace. The news of the guards' actions should be widely circulated on all media platforms, making sure that every citizen is aware of their terrorizing behaviour.

To mitigate the impact on the families of the guards, news should be released that their allowances would not be affected during the exercise. Meanwhile, demonstrations should continue all over Sikkim, with people demanding the full removal of the Chogyal.

The Indian government would ask the people of Sikkim to exercise patience and remain calm during the upcoming events.

It was crucial that the situation should not escalate into violence or chaos. Additionally, the government would take measures to ensure that the Chogyal should not run away from Sikkim. All exits should be guarded to prevent his escape. In case, he asked for asylum, he would be taken to India House for his safety.

However, the government did not want to keep the Chogyal at India House for too long, as it could lead to unnecessary tension and resentment. After a period of time, he would be transferred to a guest house located about 15-20 miles away from Gangtok. Once he was in a secure location, negotiations could begin in earnest.

It is important to note that during this time, India would also need to work on diplomatic fronts and keep the international community informed about the situation in Sikkim. The Indian government would need to assure them that the merger of Sikkim was being carried out in a peaceful and democratic manner, and that the human rights of the Sikkimese people were being protected.

It was also important to ensure that the media coverage of the events in Sikkim was controlled and monitored carefully. The government would need to communicate the message that the removal of the Sikkim guards and the eventual merger with India was necessary for the development and progress of Sikkim, and that the Chogyal was obstructing this progress.

Once the Sikkim guards were disarmed and the Chogyal was removed from power, the next step would be to prepare for the integration of Sikkim into the Indian Union. This would require the drafting and passing of new legislation, the establishment of administrative structures and institutions, and the integration of Sikkim into the Indian economy and political system.

The deployment of three army battalions under the 64 brigade marked the final stage of the plan for the merger of Sikkim with India. The swift and efficient disarmament of the Sikkim guards took less than 20 minutes. The Chogyal was understandably furious at India's move, but he was unable to do anything to resist it. He was left feeling helpless and powerless as India tightened its grip on Sikkim.

After the disarming of Sikkim guards by the Indian army, it was the perfect time for Kazi to take action and inform the people of Sikkim that their future lies with India. He saw the emergency assembly session on 10 April as the perfect opportunity to do so. 29 Sikkim Congress legislators were present at the session, and Kazi used this platform to demand the full merger of Sikkim with India.

Kazi knew that the people of Sikkim were tired of the constant political instability and the Chogyal's autocratic rule. He believed that the merger with India would bring much-needed stability and progress to Sikkim. He made a passionate speech, urging his fellow legislators and the people of Sikkim to support the merger, and to embrace the new opportunities that it would bring.

Kazi emphasized that the merger would provide the people of Sikkim with the benefits of Indian democracy, and that, Sikkim would no longer be isolated from the rest of the country. He also spoke about the economic benefits of the merger, highlighting that it would bring new industries and job opportunities to Sikkim.

The emergency assembly session was a turning point in the Sikkim merger process. Kazi's speech resonated with the people of Sikkim, and they started to see the benefits of the merger. The demand for full merger with India grew louder and more widespread.

Kazi was now the new king of Sikkim for the people.

On 11 April, the External Affairs Minister Y.B. Chavan addressed the Parliament about the ongoing situation in Sikkim. He informed the members that the Chief Minister of Sikkim had requested the disarmament of the Sikkim Guards due to the growing unrest in the state. As per the request, the army had acted upon it and disarmed the guards in the palace on 9 April afternoon.

Additionally, the Chief Minister had also called for the abolition of the Chogyal's position, and in a meeting held on 10 April, a resolution had been passed for the same.

Chavan's statement was significant as it signaled the Indian government's firm stance on the matter, and reaffirmed its commitment to the merger of Sikkim with India. The statement also highlighted the support of the Sikkim Congress and the Chief Minister's position in favour of the merger.

The statement was widely reported in the media, and it further fueled the agitation for the merger among the people of Sikkim. It also signaled to the international community that India was taking firm steps towards the integration of Sikkim with India, and was not willing to entertain any external interference in the matter.

Finally, on 15 May 1975, the Sikkim assembly passed a resolution in favour of the merger with India, and Sikkim became the 22nd state of India. Here ended RAW's 27 months involvement in the mission and the success of the operation delighted everyone involved. The overall agenda behind everything was to have a peaceful merger and the same happened as well. This became another feather in the cap of R.N. Kao and his team that worked tirelessly to achieve what seemed to be impossible at the beginning.

❑

Kao's Biggest Failure

R.N. Kao was a seasoned intelligence officer, who understood the nature of this work. Despite the successes achieved in Bangladesh and Sikkim, he knew that taking a break and enjoying the glory was not an option. Intelligence work requires relentless effort and attention, as even a single mistake can have catastrophic consequences.

The geopolitical landscape constantly chanesg, with new challenges and threats emerging on a daily basis. To stay ahead of the curve, organizations, like RAW, must work tirelessly to gather information, analyze it, and take appropriate action. This requires a high level of skill, dedication, and perseverance.

For intelligence officers like R.N. Kao, the work is never done. Even after a successful mission, there is always more to be done, as the threats and challenges facing the nation are constantly evolving. Whether it is gathering intelligence on terrorist activities, monitoring hostile foreign governments, or tracking the movements of criminal organizations, the work of an intelligence officer is never-ending.

After the 1962 Sino-Indian War, the Central Intelligence Agency (CIA) played a critical role in setting up India's external intelligence agency, the Research and Analysis Wing (RAW), and in providing assistance for a number of covert operations. However, by the early 1970s, the relationship between the CIA and India began to change.

One of the primary reasons for this shift was Pakistan. The United States began to view Pakistan as a critical partner in its efforts to contain Soviet influence in the region. As a result, the CIA sought to gain greater access to China through Pakistan, and began to see India as less of a priority.

Furthermore, the personal relationship between Indian Prime Minister Indira Gandhi and the US government began to sour. The Nixon administration was openly hostile towards Gandhi and her socialist policies, and sought to undermine her government through covert means. The US government believed that Gandhi was too close to the Soviet Union, and that her policies were detrimental to US interests in the region.

These factors led to a gradual distance between the CIA and India. While the CIA continued to provide some support to RAW and to assist in certain covert operations, the level of assistance was greatly reduced. By the end of the 1970s, the relationship between the two countries had deteriorated significantly, and would take many years to repair.

R.N. Kao, being a seasoned intelligence officer, recognized that RAW needed to improve its capabilities in predicting the movements of naval ships of major world powers, such as the United States. This was a critical area of concern, as the presence of foreign naval vessels in the Indian Ocean could have significant implications for India's national security.

Despite efforts to improve these capabilities with the help of the KGB of the Soviet Union, Kao realized that there were limitations to what they could offer. As a result, he began to explore other options, and reached out to the French intelligence agency, SDECE.

France, a major colonial power with a long history of maritime activities, had extensive experience in monitoring and predicting the movements of naval vessels. SDECE had developed sophisticated capabilities in this area, and Kao believed that they could offer valuable assistance to RAW. Kao knew that over-dependence on US would backfire one day or another, so he kept on looking for alternatives, and for this particular task, French were among the best options.

The French intelligence agency, SDECE, was headed by Count Alexandre de Marenches during the time when Kao reached out to them for cooperation. Count de Marenches was a highly respected intelligence officer, with extensive experience in intelligence operations in Asia and the Middle East.

When Kao expressed interest in working with SDECE, the French were quick to respond. They too recognized the importance of expanding their intelligence operations in Asia, and saw India as a critical partner in this endeavour.

As a result, Kao was invited to Paris to meet Count de Marenches and other senior officials at SDECE. The meeting proved to be highly productive, with Kao and de Marenches developing an instant rapport. They shared a common vision for expanding intelligence cooperation between India and France, and worked closely together to develop a strategy for achieving this goal.

The intelligence cooperation between RAW and SDECE proved to be highly effective in monitoring the movements of foreign naval vessels in the Indian Ocean. With the help of the

French, RAW was able to obtain real-time intelligence on not just US ships, but also on Soviet vessels operating in the region.

This intelligence cooperation was highly valued by the French, who saw it as an opportunity to expand their intelligence network in Asia. To this end, Count de Marenches suggested that RAW should consider bringing the Iranian Intelligence Agency, SAVAK, into the partnership.

SAVAK was known to have extensive intelligence capabilities in the Middle East, and had a wealth of information on Soviet and American activities in the region. Kao recognized the potential benefits of including SAVAK in the partnership and agreed to explore this option further.

Despite some initial reservations from RAW about working with SAVAK, Kao was able to persuade his colleagues of the importance of this partnership. With the help of the French, RAW was able to establish a working relationship with SAVAK, which proved to be highly successful.

The trilateral arrangement between France, Iran, and India involved a division of labor where each country contributed its strengths to the partnership. Iran provided funding for the acquisition of technical equipment and France supplied the necessary technical expertise and equipment, while India contributed its trained manpower to operate the equipment.

Under this arrangement, France acquired advanced technical equipment and software, which they provided to India for use in intelligence operations. Iran funded the purchase of this equipment, and provided financial support for the partnership.

India, in turn, provided highly trained personnel, who were skilled in operating the advanced equipment provided by France. These personnel worked closely with their French and Iranian counterparts to collect and analyze intelligence data.

The results of these intelligence operations were shared among all three partners, allowing each country to benefit from the information obtained. This trilateral arrangement proved to be highly effective in expanding the intelligence capabilities of all three countries, and strengthening their partnerships in the field of intelligence.

B. Raman was chosen by R.N. Kao to serve as a covert intelligence operative in Paris under the guise of a journalist. Raman was selected for the job due to his expertise in journalism, having studied the field, and worked at the Indian Express for several years. He had a solid understanding of the workings of the media industry, and was therefore a natural fit for this role.

Raman's assignment lasted for four years, from 1975 to 1979, during which time he played a critical role in setting up two intelligence stations on the east and west coasts of India. These stations were tasked with monitoring foreign naval vessels in the Indian Ocean, particularly those of the United States and the Soviet Union.

Raman's work in Paris was highly valued by RAW, and was considered crucial in strengthening the agency's intelligence-gathering capabilities. However, the partnership between France, Iran, and India came to an abrupt end, when the Iranian government was toppled in 1979.

Despite the setback faced by RAW in the Iran-France-India intelligence cooperation, the agency was on the rise during the 1970s under the leadership of R.N. Kao. Kao's success in Bangladesh and Sikkim had earned him the trust and confidence of Prime Minister Indira Gandhi, who relied heavily on him to bolster India's intelligence capabilities.

RAW was becoming a highly popular organization among the youth of India, and Kao recognized the need to recruit bright young talent to meet the agency's expanding responsibilities. He began to directly recruit candidates from colleges and universities, through a rigorous selection process to ensure that only the best and brightest were chosen.

The selection process for RAW was extremely selective, with candidates required to fill out a 35-page application form that delved into every aspect of their background. Once the initial screening was complete, candidates were subjected to a series of tests, often held at odd hours. like 3 a.m., to gauge their aptitude and suitability for intelligence work. Those who passed these tests then proceeded to individual interviews, which were conducted over multiple levels and could last for hours.

The interviews were designed to test the candidate's knowledge, intelligence, critical thinking, and problem-solving abilities. The questions asked could cover a wide range of topics, including politics, economics, history, and current affairs. Only those who demonstrated exceptional abilities and the potential for success in the field of intelligence were chosen.

In 1975, RAW faced a challenging year, marked by both successes and failures. While RAW played a significant role in the liberation of Bangladesh in 1971, it was unable to prevent the brutal assassination of Sheikh Mujibur Rahman, the country's first president, and his family on August 15, 1975. Mujibur Rahman, his wife, three sons, and two daughters were brutally killed in the coup d'état that overthrew the government. Only his two daughters, Sheikh Hasina and Sheikh Rehana, survived as they were abroad at the time.

The assassination of Mujibur Rahman and his family was a severe setback for RAW, as it raised questions about the agency's ability to gather intelligence and act effectively on it. RAW was criticized for not detecting the conspiracy in time and failing to warn the Bangladeshi authorities, despite having a significant intelligence presence in the country. The incident also damaged India's relationship with Bangladesh, which had previously been a strong ally.

The assassination of Mujibur Rahman and his family was a tragic event, and RAW learned valuable lessons from it.

The main reason behind this failure of RAW was loss of contact because of the sudden death of P.N. Banerjee in Dhaka hotel in July 1974. Banerjee had the network that was the ear and eye of Kao and RAW in Bangladesh, and when he died, it was difficult for RAW to regain the lost vision.

But, there were other reasons as well. There were many instances where Mujibur was warned by RAW, even twice by Kao himself, but he never took the warnings seriously. Kao wondered that how can RAW be considered at fault if Mujibur himself is not taking the warnings seriously.

As RAW was trying to come out of the failure of Mujibur, next big thing happened and this time it was because of Mrs. Gandhi—the Emergency. The Emergency, which lasted from 1975 to 1977, was a dark period in Indian history. It was imposed by Prime Minister Indira Gandhi after a court declared her 1971 election to the Lok Sabha invalid due to electoral malpractices. Her younger son, Sanjay Gandhi, who wielded enormous influence over his mother, is said to have advised her to declare an emergency in order to maintain her grip on power.

During the Emergency, civil liberties were suspended, the press was censored, and political opponents were arrested and jailed without trial. It was a period of repression and authoritarianism, and it led to widespread criticism both within India and abroad.

Even Kao had no knowledge of this beforehand. It happened all of a sudden. She felt paranoid about many situations. She thought that CIA was behind her and her family. She believed no one. When the news of Mujibur's assassination came to Gandhi's ear, she lost all her senses. The ruthless killing of the leader and his family including the nine year old son of Mujibur, somewhat shook her.

According to intelligence reports, Mrs. Gandhi's concerns regarding her personal safety were not unfounded. Although the threat did not come from foreign powers, there were internal threats to her life. The death of Mujibur added to her fears, and she was apprchensive about the security of her family and herself. The intelligence community supported her fears, and they had information regarding a potential threat to her life.

Mrs. Gandhi was deeply affected by the brutal killing of Mujibur and his family. She was particularly disturbed by the fact that Mujibur's son was of the same age as her own grandson, Rahul. The thought of such violence being inflicted on innocent children kept her up at night, and intensified her fear of internal threats to her own family and the country as a whole.

Sanjay Gandhi's interference in matters that were beyond his purview became a problem for Kao, the head of RAW. Sanjay, who held no position in the government, began to demand access to appointment files, which was unconstitutional. This created a headache for Kao and added to the already existing tension.

Before the announcement of the Emergency, Mrs. Gandhi requested Kao to appoint his close associate, Nair, as the Director of IB. However, Kao reminded her that Nair had previously refused the post twice, and was content with his current position in RAW. Mrs. Gandhi, however, did not take no for an answer this time, and Nair was appointed as the Director of IB.

Days before the Emergency period, Sanjay Gandhi began to question the loyalty of DIB Nair, who had been appointed on Mrs. Gandhi's request. One evening, Mrs. Gandhi summoned Nair to her residence, but he refused to go, as he only met with the PM in the office and that too rarely. Sanjay Gandhi was infuriated by Nair's refusal, and questioned the appointment of such a person as DIB.

The following day, Nair was informed that his promotion as DIB had been cancelled. To Nair's relief, he was happy to hear the news, as he had not wanted the promotion in the first place.

During the Emergency period, RAW had to work under immense pressure and constant surveillance from the government.

Kao and Nair tried their best to keep RAW out of the political turmoil and keep its operations focused on external intelligence gathering. However, with the change in government in 1977, RAW faced a new set of challenges.

Morarji Desai, the new Prime Minister of India, had a different approach towards intelligence agencies. He believed in reducing their powers and limiting their scope of operations. He ordered a review of all intelligence agencies, including RAW, and sought to bring them under greater scrutiny and control.

This created a difficult situation for RAW, as it had to navigate between its mandate of gathering external intelligence, and the government's demand for greater accountability and transparency. The agency had to work hard to regain the trust of the new government, and prove its worth as a vital component of India's national security apparatus.

RAW had to adapt to the changing political scenario and the evolving security threats facing India. The agency had to realign its priorities and find new ways to gather intelligence, while staying within the boundaries set by the government.

Kao was deeply hurt by Morarji Desai's distrust towards RAW. He believed that RAW was an important agency that played a crucial role in safeguarding India's national security interests. However, Morarji Desai was a firm believer in transparency, and had a different approach towards governance. He was critical of the secretive nature of intelligence agencies, and believed that they should be made accountable to the government.

During the reign of Morarji Desai as the Prime Minister of India, he was advised to appoint Nair as the secretary of RAW. However, Nair did not find the working conditions suitable, and decided to resign within three months of his appointment. Despite Morarji's attempts to persuade him to stay, Nair stood firm on his principles and left the post. This departure left the organization in a state of grief, and there was a sense of abandonment on the occasion of its 10th anniversary. Nair was highly respected by his colleagues for his dedication to his work and his aversion to politics interfering with it. Nevertheless, Kao had trained the RAW officers well and others were ready to take control, including N.F. Suntook. His appointment as the new chief was a stroke of luck for RAW.

Narayan F. Suntook, or N.F. Suntook, had an impressive background before becoming the Chief of RAW. He had joined the Indian Police Service in 1955, and served in various positions before being handpicked by Rameshwar Nath Kao to join RAW in 1968.

During his tenure in RAW, Suntook held various positions, including Deputy Chief and Chief of Station in several countries. He was known for his analytical and strategic thinking skills, as well as his ability to build strong relationships with intelligence agencies of other countries.

Suntook was also involved in some of the most significant intelligence operations of RAW. For instance, he played a crucial role in the creation of the Bangladesh's 'Mukti Bahini' during the Bangladesh Liberation War in 1971, which led to the formation of Bangladesh.

Apart from his work in RAW, Suntook was also known for his literary pursuits. He was a prolific writer and had authored several books, including "The Second Scandal of the Century," a novel based on a real-life financial scam.

After Nair's resignation, the post of RAW Chief was left vacant. The newly-elected Prime Minister of India, Morarji Desai, was not a big fan of the agency. However, he was advised to appoint N.F. Suntook as the new RAW Chief, whom he had seen in action during his tenure as Chief Minister of Maharashtra.

Suntook was known for his low profile, but highly effective leadership skills during his tenure in the Bombay Police. Despite being initially reluctant to take up the post, Suntook eventually accepted the role of RAW Chief, and it proved to be a turning point for the agency. When Suntook took over, RAW was in a state of crisis and was on the verge of collapse due to a lack of direction and leadership.

Suntook became the anchor that RAW needed at that time. He restructured the organization, bringing in new talent and implementing effective strategies. Under his leadership, RAW regained its strength and credibility. Suntook focused on strengthening the agency's intelligence-gathering capabilities and improving coordination with other intelligence agencies.

During Suntook's tenure as RAW chief, he had to face challenges, not just from outside, but also from within the government. Two of the ministers in the Morarji Desai cabinet were not fond of Kao, and the reason behind this was their belief that it was Kao who had advised Mrs. Gandhi to impose the Emergency. These ministers were Charan Singh and Atal Bihari Vajpayee, who were known for their suspicion towards intelligence agencies.

To address their concerns, a thorough inquiry was conducted by the Home Ministry to clear any doubts about Kao's role during the Emergency period. After the inquiry, the two ministers reversed their decision on Kao.

However, the situation didn't change much as Morarji Desai cut 50% of RAW's budget, which created a lot of challenges for Suntook.

In 1977, Suntook discovered that the MEA bureaucracy was attempting to persuade India to join the NPT (Nuclear Non-Proliferation Treaty), which was not in India's best interests. Suntook recognized the significance of this issue, and had to convey this to the Prime Minister, Morarji Desai. However, he understood that Desai would be unwilling to listen to him. There was only one person who had the authority to persuade Desai, and that was the renowned Indian scientist, Dr. Homi Sethna.

However, Sethna would only listen to Kao. Kao and Sethna had a close friendship during Mrs. Gandhi's administration, which Suntook knew about. As a result, he sought Kao's assistance in persuading Sethna to intervene in the matter.

Kao was not as prominent as he had been previously, but his expertise was still required in RAW. Suntook, being aware of this, understood that he could rely on Kao's network and knowledge to navigate through such difficult situations. Kao's friendship with Sethna proved to be invaluable in convincing him to talk to Desai, and persuade him not to join the NPT. This small contribution of Kao made a wonderful impact on India's history. If NPT would have been signed by India, there would have been no nuclear weapon, and we would have never experienced the meaning of freesom as we understand it now.

During Morarji's tenure as the Prime Minister of India, he had a change of heart, and realized the importance of intelligence agencies like RAW for the progress and security of developing countries like India. However, this realization came too late, as his shortsightedness had already left a deep scar on the history of RAW.

Morarji's initial lack of trust in RAW and its officers had caused a significant setback to the organization's growth and reputation. His decision to cut the budget of RAW by 50% had caused widespread panic and left the organization on the brink of failure. Additionally, his suspicion of Kao and his role in the emergency had created a rift between the government and the intelligence agency.

After Mrs. Indira Gandhi's return to power in 1980, she once again showed her faith in R.N. Kao, but she also valued N.F. Suntook's leadership and decided to keep him as the Chief of RAW. When she took the power, she started to remove chiefs of IB and the CBI, so it was normal to think that she would replace Suntook as well because he was also appointed by Desai, but she took Kao's advice and then retained Suntook at the post of Chief of RAW. However, she also appointed Kao as a senior advisor of the Cabinet Secretariat. The combination of Kao's experience and Suntook's effective leadership proved to be a winning one for RAW.

During this time, Kao and Suntook worked closely together to address the issues that were left unresolved in RAW during Kao's absence. Kao's experience and expertise in the field of intelligence proved to be invaluable, as he provided guidance and support to Suntook and other officers of RAW.

During Mrs. Gandhi's second term in power, four officers of RAW were accused of being involved in plotting against her and were subjected to humiliation. Despite Kao's influence, he was unable to save them and they were sent back to their respective states with their promotions reversed. One of the officers, Shiv Raj, was a beloved low-profile figure, whom Kao had a particular fondness for. Unfortunately, even Kao's support was not enough to protect him from Mrs. Gandhi's wrath.

1980 was a very bad year for RAW. There were so many challenges to counter within the organization itself. There was a clear divide between senior and junior officers. Juniors used to think that seniors do not care about the difficulties that the juniors are facing. There was no clear line or transparency regarding the promotions, transfers, etc.

The regular inspections conducted by CI&S (Counter Intelligence and Security) had a negative impact on the morale of the lower and middle-class staff of RAW. The inspections were carried out without proper documentation and the inspectors often behaved rudely with the staff. The treatment meted out by the inspectors was always questionable, as they didn't show the same strictness with senior officers. This created a sense of mistrust among the lower and middle-class staff, who felt that the organization believed that they were the only ones who would create problems within the organization and needed to be kept under regular surveillance.

These inspections not only affected the morale of the staff, but also led to a sense of fear and distrust. The staff felt they were being unfairly targeted, while senior officers were getting a free pass. This created a rift within the organization and affected the overall efficiency of RAW. The lack of trust and cooperation between different staff levels affected the organization's functioning, which was detrimental to the national interest.

Once during these surveys conducted by CI&S, the staff of RAW became angry, and they declared a strike. The Delhi Police had to get to the matter to rescue the team of CI&S. Mrs. Gandhi should have thought that Suntook was not able to impart discipline to his staff, but she didn't give it much thought. The main reason for it was the involvement of Kao. It took time for Suntook to get things under control. But once things got in control, he started to think beyond. He used the unrest in Pakistan after the assassination of ZA Bhutto and started to build a network within Pakistan which was helped by Kao in many ways. He gave many of his own sources to Suntook to get to the very base of Pakistan. This was the time when Pakistan was trying to make and test their nuclear power.

In the 1980s, India faced a major security challenge in the form of the Khalistan movement in Punjab. The Khalistan movement was an insurgent movement seeking to create a separate Sikh state in Punjab. The movement was fueled by a number of factors, including religious and economic grievances, as well as a sense of discrimination against Sikhs by the Indian state.

RAW played a key role in addressing the Khalistan problem in Punjab. The agency used a combination of intelligence gathering, covert operations, and psychological warfare to counter the Khalistan militants and to undermine their morale. RAW also worked closely with the Indian Army, which had been deployed in Punjab to maintain law and order.

One of the critical challenges faced by RAW in Punjab was to distinguish between the genuine grievances of the Sikh community and the violent activities of the Khalistan militants. The agency used a variety of intelligence gathering techniques to infiltrate the Khalistan movement and identify its leaders and supporters.

Despite the efforts of RAW and the Indian security forces, the Khalistan movement continued to pose a significant security threat to India for much of the 1980s.

Things then became ugly with Operation Blue star. Operation Blue Star, which was the code name for the Indian Army's operation to enter the Golden Temple complex in Amritsar in June 1984, was a turning point in the Sikh separatist movement in India. The operation was aimed at flushing out Sikh militants who had fortified themselves inside the Golden Temple complex, but it resulted in significant loss of life and damage to the temple. Many Sikhs saw this as an attack on their religion and an infringement of their rights, which led to widespread anger and protests in the Sikh community.

The anger took such a shape that on October 31, 1984, two of Indira Gandhi's bodyguards who were Sikh, assassinated her at her residence in New Delhi in retaliation for the Indian Army's operation on the Golden Temple. The assassination triggered widespread riots against the Sikh community, resulting in the deaths of thousands of Sikhs.

Prior to 1975, the division in the Intelligence Bureau (IB) responsible for the security of the Prime Minister was a relatively small outfit comprising only three officers. However, the situation changed after the declaration of Emergency in India in 1975, which resulted in the imposition of severe restrictions on civil liberties and the increased centralization of power.

Given the heightened security threats to then-Prime Minister Indira Gandhi, the division responsible for her security was expanded and strengthened. Additionally, another group that was perceived to pose a threat to the Prime Minister's safety was the 'Anand Marg', a Hindu spiritual organization with a significant international following.

As a result, the IB increased its surveillance and monitoring activities on the Anand Marg and other similar groups to ensure the safety and security of the Prime Minister and other top leaders. The expansion of the security apparatus also reflected the growing realization that the threats to the safety of India's leaders had become more complex and multifaceted in the wake of the Emergency.

Kao recognized the importance of ensuring the safety and security of the Prime Minister of India during foreign visits, and thus, he established a special unit within RAW called the VIP Security Division. This division was tasked with gathering intelligence on potential threats to the Prime Minister's safety during foreign visits and implementing appropriate security measures to mitigate those threats. The VIP Security Division worked closely with the Intelligence Bureau's Special Branch, which was responsible for the Prime Minister's security within India. Together, these two agencies played a crucial role in ensuring the safety of India's political leadership both within the country and abroad.

When Mrs Gandhi was facing threats from all around the world, it was imperative for RAW to take necessary actions to ensure her safety. And for that, Kao brainstormed with his colleagues to get things done. Blueprints of various circumstances were made, and the solutions were ready on paper. Then came the execution part, which had its own set of problems. But Kao was ready for everything.

The division was faced with a significant challenge when it came to providing Mrs. Gandhi with a bulletproof car. As there was no car manufacturing company in India that could make a bulletproof Ambassador, the cars were sent to Germany for bulletproofing. Mrs. Gandhi, who preferred to travel in Indian cars, was not initially happy with this arrangement. Kao also ensured that an ambulance, with a doctor and nurse ready, was always present in the convoy. Although Mrs. Gandhi was not comfortable with the sight of an ambulance stationed outside her house at all times, Kao made sure that it was stationed at a distance but always in convoy.

The third and perhaps most challenging decision made by Kao was to persuade Mrs. Gandhi to wear a bulletproof vest. This required a great deal of courage, as no one had dared to ask for her size. Kao took the blouse of a woman on the staff, who was nearly the same size as Mrs. Gandhi, and used it to make three vests of the same size. After a great deal of persuasion, Mrs. Gandhi eventually agreed to wear the vest, although she was irregular in doing so.

When the assassination of Indira Gandhi took place, R.N. Kao was not in India, but on a mission in China as per Mrs. Gandhi's instructions. She had tasked Kao with strengthening the relations between India and China. Upon hearing about the tragedy, the Chinese authorities arranged for a special plane to bring Kao back to India as soon as possible.

Kao's return to India after the assassination of Mrs. Gandhi must have been a difficult time for him. As the founder of RAW and a trusted advisor to Mrs. Gandhi, he may have felt that he had failed in his duty to protect her. However, Kao was a private person who never talked about his personal feelings or experiences in public.

Although there were failures attached to his life, his successes were so huge that everything can be ignored. Till today, Rameshwar Nath Kao is widely regarded as one of the greatest intelligence officers in Indian history, and is often credited with establishing and building India's external intelligence agency, RAW, into a world-class organization. His strategic thinking, organizational skills, and ability to recruit and retain talented officers were instrumental in the success of RAW in gathering intelligence, and carrying out covert operations in some of the most challenging regions of the world. Kao's contributions to India's national security and foreign policy are immeasurable, and his legacy lives on in the agency he helped create.

❑❑❑